WHAT READERS ARE SAYING ABOUT

Thoughtbooks

"Original techniques instead of recycled information, making it a valuable resource for personal growth." – *MB*

"It feels like it's talking directly to you, breaking down complex ideas in a super accessible way. It's eye-opening and gave me real tools to think clearly without feeling overwhelmed." – *Sam F.*

"A refreshing, straightforward approach to help you regain control over your thoughts, without overcomplicating the process. A must-read book!" – *Lauren P.*

"A practical and valuable resource for anyone looking to work on their mindset." – *S. Y.*

"Well-written from a practical point of view." – *Steve G.*

"The strategies are easy to follow, and the tone is refreshingly down-to-earth—no fluff, just real tips that work" – *Amazon Reviewer*

"A surprisingly genuine and honest read that cuts through a lot of the noise that surrounds this genre." – *Vince*

"I love this book!" – *Amazon Reviewer*

"I appreciate how this book is great at validating you at whatever step of the process you are at!" – *Goodreads Reviewer*

"Packed with useful new information I hadn't come across before. There's a simple method offered to do a reset and cultivate a new mindset, and I am enthusiastically applying it. Really an excellent book!" – *Analogica*

"There is much fascinating "food for thought" here, and in fact, I intend to go back and review the core of the book again ... and probably will do so regularly."
– *Jamie B.*

"This book has already benefited me as I move into a new position at work that puts me out of my comfort zone. I have legit been using the ICE method and utilizing the different rules to help mitigate a lot of my spiraling or ruminating thoughts." – *Goodreads Reviewer*

middle think

/ noun /

---

finding a space between extremes and recognizing life's nuances and complexities—even when it's challenging or inconvenient.

Middle
Think

Middle Think

The Life-Changing Skill of Overcoming Extreme Thoughts

Lyndsey Getty

Thought
Method
Company

for us

"The middle path is the best path. "
– *Buddha*

"In the middle of difficulty lies opportunity."
– *Albert Einstein*

"Balance is not something you find, it's something you create."
– *Jana Kingsford*

Contents

Middle Think in an Infomercial

The infomercial opens with a montage of people in various relatable situations.

An anxious partygoer clutches their drink, watching others chat and laugh. Their inner voice, pessimistic and defeated, plays over the scene: *Everyone else is happy and connected. I'll never make friends.*

The overwhelmed couch potato sits surrounded by clutter. They flip through TV channels, feeling hopeless. Their internal dialogue cuts through the faint sound of the news: *I'm unproductive and lazy. I'll never get out of this rut.*

A midnight overthinker lies in bed, their mind racing between global worries and replaying an argument with an ex: *Everything is doomed. I ruin my relationships. My ex was perfect. I'll never move on.*

Three columns appear on the screen showing each person in their moment of struggle. A narrator's voice, empathetic and encouraging, asks: "Do you ever feel like everything is either perfect or a disaster? Like no matter what you do, it's never enough? That nothing will ever get better? These thoughts can be overwhelming, but you're not alone. There is a way out."

The screen shifts to a peaceful, well-lit room. A presenter, calm and relatable, smiles warmly at the camera. "We've all been there. The constant barrage of extreme thoughts, negative news, and pressure to be perfect can leave us feeling anxious, depressed, and sleep deprived. But what if I told you there was a way to escape the cycle? Introducing Middle Thinking—a revolutionary thought process that helps you let go of extremes and find balance." Presenter confidently walks toward the camera. "With middle thinking, you'll learn how to stop your mind from going to extremes. No more catastrophizing every little setback, or feeling paralyzed by perfectionism. Instead, you'll embrace balance and find clarity." The camera follows the presenter to a corner of the room where people are reading the book *Middle Think*. The presenter moves through the area, observing the readers. One person does guided exercises, while another has a thought bubble with the extreme thought, *Nothing ever works out*, transform into a more balanced one, *Some things may go wrong, but others will work out*. The camera focuses on a third person. Their internal monologue is heard, saying, "I'm not alone. There's a way to change this!"

With an inviting smile, the presenter walks back to their initial position, camera following, "With *Middle Think*, you'll learn to identify extreme thoughts and shift to a more productive, balanced mindset."

The screen transitions to a montage of the earlier situations, revealing each person's experience after learning to Middle Think.

The anxious partygoer is enjoying the atmosphere, starting a conversation with a stranger without the pressure to be perfect. The couch potato declutters a corner of their living room, relieved by the idea of taking small steps. And the midnight overthinker sleeps peacefully, understanding that they can build healthy relationships and not every thought is a crisis.

The presenter concludes: "Don't let another day slip by feeling overwhelmed or stuck. Join the thousands of people who have already transformed their lives with *Middle Think*."

Serene music plays as the screen fades to a peaceful landscape, showing a pyramid of *Middle Think* books and ordering information. The final narration says: "Learn the life-changing skill of identifying and overcoming extreme thoughts with middle thinking. Start your journey to a more peaceful mind today."

Middle Think Is a New Beginning

We all feel overwhelmed by our thoughts, but many of us don't realize we're thinking in extremes and how much those extremes affect us. Also known as "all-or-nothing" or "black-and-white" thinking, extreme thoughts can seem normal because they're common and encouraged in our environment. But these thoughts are far from normal. They create an inner turmoil that leads to hopelessness, anxiety, stress, and are a major cause of depression.[1]

A result of extreme thinking is perfectionism. So when we sense something is off, we often blame ourselves instead of questioning the extreme thoughts. This is often why people describe themselves as "broken." And if someone ever told you—or you thought to yourself—that you "just need to toughen up," well, that's a commonly accepted extreme belief.[2]

Similar to outdated laws and mindsets, just because something is widely believed doesn't mean it's healthy. Could you imagine if people still believed smoking was harmless?[3] If people recognized the negative impact of extremes, there would be a public health advisory and a major shift in attitudes.[4]

Sadly, most of us don't realize we're thinking in extremes, how much these intense thoughts hold us back, and that they're destroying our happiness. Even if someone recognizes that extremes are negatively affecting them, there aren't any resources to help.

Coping tools that don't address the root cause, and advice to think "with balance" are too generic and ambiguous to make an impact. To make actual change, we need a healthy model to influence and inspire us; a method we can follow so we can challenge extremes and build the life-changing skill of finding a balanced perspective. I call this framework "middle think" or "middle thinking," and it's what you will learn here.

Middle think can be used synonymously with "balance" and since balance is a recognized concept, I will use them interchangeably. But it's important to recognize that balance doesn't mean achieving a perfect state (defining balance that way is a side effect of perfectionism and extreme thinking). Instead, balance is about finding a space between extremes and recognizing life's nuances and complexities—even when it's challenging or inconvenient.

Here you will learn to recognize extreme thought patterns and overcome them by creating a balanced, middle thinking mindset. Since your surroundings play a significant role in shaping your thought habits, throughout the book I will describe what it would be like to live in a more balanced world, "The Middle."

The first half of the book will help you uncover extremes in your environment and show you how to middle think. The second half offers fresh perspectives and practical exercises to help you continue finding your middle. After the main content, I've also included templates and bonus material for those, like me, who enjoy that kind of stuff.

I love when authors keep things simple and to the point, so there's a lot of information condensed into short sections. Take breaks to let information sink in as needed. This is a reference for you, so don't be shy in revisiting the sections you need most.

Lastly, please read this in a conversational tone, knowing it's meant to be supportive. My goal is to share insights and encouragement to help you develop balanced thoughts. I have firsthand experience with the stress and pressure of extremes. And I learned that true strength comes from challenging all-or-nothing and embracing life's nuances. This process isn't easy, but if I've made it less overwhelming for you, then this book has achieved its purpose.

Middle Think Is a Saturday Afternoon Case Study

In the infomercial we saw what extreme thinking looks like in various situations. Now let's see how a day filled with extreme environmental influences turns out.

Kai spent his morning checking things off his to-do list. Feeling good about his progress, he took a break to eat some fruit and scroll on his phone. His news feed was full of depressing headlines: "You'll Never Afford a House,"[5] "No One Is Safe,"[6] and "Nobody Wants Relationships Anymore."[7]

Frustrated, he switched over to social media. A health influencer preached about cutting out all sugar and carbs, while another was listing out what "every woman wants in a man." The posts were full of arguments and judgmental comments.

While Kai discovered some uplifting videos, his mind wandered, questioning whether the sugar in the raspberries he was eating would negatively impact his diet. His phone vibrated in his hand; it was a text from a friend suggesting Kai's new partner is cheating since they didn't reply to his text last night.

Needing a break, Kai turned on some music. The first song had lyrics like "You ain't nobody 'til you got somebody."[8] Already disappointed that his new partner wasn't responding and, according to his friend, was cheating, Kai turned off the music, put away the berries, and ordered a burger and fries.

His phone vibrated again. He eagerly checked his notifications hoping it was a reassuring message from his partner, but it was his mom asking if he got a promotion.

Poor Kai. Yesterday he was told that if he didn't increase his productivity at work, he would need to get his resume ready. Already stressed, he thought he was doing good by trying to have a productive weekend. Now he feels like a nobody, guilty for breaking his diet, worried about his relationship, reminded of his work failings, confused about healthy foods, and stressed about the future. The burger and fries couldn't come soon enough.

If Kai Lived in The Middle

In The Middle, people perceive everyday experiences with nuance. Here, Kai wouldn't have to deal with dramatic headlines. Instead of bleak stories, he would see news that reports facts. He would understand that despite the challenging market, it's still possible to buy a house.[9] Aware of violence, he would know that overall, crime rates are going down.[10] And he'd see that dating can be hard, but people still find loving partners.[11]

On social media, influencers would share different ways to reach diet goals, admitting there's no one-size-fits-all solution and sharing their personal struggles. And they wouldn't classify all sugar as bad, noting that fruit contains sugar, but it's not the same as the refined sugars found in processed foods, making it part of a balanced, nutritious diet.[12] Instead of lists like "what women want," advice would focus on qualities like kindness, loyalty, and love, outlining that relationships need strong foundations of trust and communication.

Commenters on posts would share their experiences without hostility. They might say, "I understand your perspective, but based on my experience..." This civil disagreement enables them to use social media as intended: to connect with others and gain insight into different viewpoints.

While Kai would be frustrated about his partner not responding to him, Kai's friend wouldn't jump to conclusions about Kai's partner cheating. Instead, he'd suggest the partner might just be bad at texting or forgetful, encouraging Kai to consider if the relationship works for him. As for music, Kai might hear lyrics about feeling unloved, but he'd know it was just artistic expression, not his reality.

In this balanced world, Kai wouldn't feel the need to escape work troubles because his conversation with his boss wasn't a threat to get his resume ready. Instead, Kai and his manager would sit on the same side of the table, discussing expectations, areas of improvement, and how his boss could better support Kai.

When his mom called, she may be eager to hear about his career progress. However, she'd ask Kai how he felt about his week, showing she cares about his well-being, not expecting him to get promoted within a couple months of starting a new job.

In The Middle, Kai would know that life isn't so intense, and his relationship status didn't define his worth. He would be proud of his productive morning, relieved to have support from his boss, and excited about this delicious burger knowing it wouldn't ruin his entire diet. And he'd eat it because he wanted to, not out of shame. While he might feel guilty about not eating the fruit, Kai wouldn't beat himself up. He'd freeze it for a smoothie another day, knowing he could add fruit to his routine over time.

Making Your Middle

Let's face it: most of us are more like Kai than we'd like to admit. We're influenced by a world of extremes and exposed to negativity, anxiety-inducing news stories, and unrealistic expectations. Even when we try our best to find balance, others can drag us down.

Kai's friend suggesting that "everybody cheats" is a rigid and depressing outlook. Kai might believe he will not find a loyal partner even if he values loyalty in relationships. And Kai's mother expecting him to be promoted within a few months is a lot of pressure. No wonder Kai is stressed and underperforming at work—having to walk on eggshells is counterproductive and hampers creativity.

If Kai lived in a more balanced world, he could breathe and have space for joy and growth. He might even have a different job, depending on if the extreme expectations led him to his current one. Kai might not even read the news because he sees a nightly unbiased news roundup and only checks social media to see what his friends have been up to.

Since our environment won't immediately change, we need to focus on finding our middle by prioritizing content that is balanced and encouraging middle thinking in those around us. Let's reference Kai's story as we talk more about extremes and learn how to middle think.

Middle Think Is
Unpacking Extremes

To think with balance, it's important to understand extreme, all-or-nothing thinking, how it affects you, and where it comes from.

Your thoughts are a powerful resource. They shape your emotions, decisions, and how you use your time, energy, and money. Frequent extreme thinking makes life harder than it needs to be. It distorts your perspective, making things seem overwhelmingly negative and unmanageable.

All-or-nothing thinking might sound new to you, but it's been influencing your life since you were little. As a kid, you may have learned that being "selfless" was "good," and anything else made you "bad." This extreme perspective ignores complexity and will lead you to disregard your own needs, constantly putting others first, and feeling guilty any time you prioritize yourself, ultimately draining your energy and self-worth.

Or maybe you felt pressured to like what everyone else liked out of fear that *no one* would like you. With this narrow outlook you're afraid to express your genuine desires, constantly seeking external validation, and struggling to form authentic connections because you're not being yourself.

Or perhaps you were told to lower your standards or give up on a dream because you'd *never* achieve it. This extreme belief prevents you from starting a new hobby or pursuing a goal that could bring you fulfillment and happiness. If you choose to ignore the extremes and pursue your desires, you will then face the pressure to be perfect, or the extremes in your environment might have led you to believe that you need numerous products or natural talent to succeed.

This will leave you overwhelmed, causing you to give up before you even begin. Ignoring your interests leads to discouragement and wasted time on unproductive activities like binge-watching or excessive drinking. You sit and watch others achieve while feeling stuck, lazy, and unproductive.

Extreme thinking also affects your relationships. If you believe the rigid idea that a romantic relationship is your only path to happiness, you may settle for unhealthy partners just to avoid being alone, ultimately leading to resentment. Extremes also make it harder to form new relationships. Someone who thinks *no one wants to date anymore* will struggle to connect with someone who is open to love. And we've all seen how extreme views can tear families and friendships apart.

Parents, for example, might feel justified in cutting off their children because of extreme beliefs about who their children should love or what career they should pursue. Since we're taught that family is *everything*, this leaves the child feeling like they have only two options: live a lie or disappoint everyone.

Extreme thinking can make different perspectives seem like a threat. Surrounding yourself only with people who share your views limits your ability to grow and makes your worldview rigid. You might start by sharing a common belief, but when you connect with others solely based on rigid beliefs, you end up agreeing to ideas you don't believe in, just to fit in—getting pushed further into harmful or dangerous thinking.[13]

Rigid beliefs don't just affect your mental health—they affect your physical health too. If you accept the common, extreme belief that "everything causes cancer," you might not bother making healthy food choices. While processed foods are convenient and delicious, they lack nutrition and can lead to heart disease and other illnesses.[14] If you think all-or-nothing regarding weight loss and jump into an intense workout routine instead of easing into it, you're more likely to get injured, burn out, or give up, which is why most diets fail.[15]

Common Cognitive Distortions

All-or-Nothing Thinking Viewing situations in black-or-white terms with no middle ground. "If I'm not perfect, I've failed."	**Mental Filtering** Focusing only on the negative aspects, ignoring the positive. "I made one mistake, so the entire presentation was terrible."
Overgeneralization Drawing broad conclusions from a single incident. "I didn't get the job; I'll never be successful."	**Discounting the Positive** Dismissing positive experiences as unimportant. "They praised me, but they were just being nice."
Jumping to Conclusions Assuming negative outcomes without evidence. "They didn't text back. They must be mad at me."	**Catastrophizing** Expecting the worst possible outcome in a situation. "I failed this test. I'll never graduate."
Magnification/Minimization Exaggerating the negative, downplaying the positive. "Yes, I finished the marathon, but I was so slow compared to others."	**Should Statements** Using rigid expectations that lead to guilt or frustration. "I should be married and have kids by the time I'm [insert age]."
Labeling Assigning negative labels to oneself or others. "I made a mistake, so I'm a failure."	**Personalization** Taking responsibility for things outside your control. "They are upset. I must have said something wrong."
Blaming Holding others responsible for your emotional state. "I'm unhappy because my friend isn't supportive."	**Emotional Reasoning** Believing that emotions reflect reality. "I feel anxious, so something bad must be happening."

All-or-nothing thinking is one of several thought patterns tied to depression and anxiety, first identified by psychologist Aaron T. Beck as "cognitive distortions."[16] Though there's a subtle difference between extreme thinking and all-or-nothing thinking, we'll use the terms interchangeably here for simplicity.

Where Extremes Come From

Extremes have been deep set in the human experience for thousands of years, with signs of extreme thinking in ancient texts going back over 2,500 years[17] and the all-or-nothing thinking idea that "no one wants to work anymore," being recycled for over a century, with some references dating back to 1894.[18]

Extreme thinking is so ingrained in our environment, polarized views, and an "us vs them" mentality are the norm. Direct influences in our lives, such as our parents, family, and teachers, as well as indirect influences like social media, TV, movies, books, celebrities, and influencers, condition us to think in extremes.

This starts in early childhood with fixed gender rules that determine what colors we're allowed to wear, toys we're allowed to play with, and things we may like. In school, rigid grading systems define us, praised only for perfect performance and punished for minor mistakes. These early experiences shape our perceptions and set the stage for how we view ourselves and the world as we grow older, adopting the extreme either/or perspective that effort and progress don't matter—there is only winning or losing, success or failure.

Then there is the constant peer pressure to follow trends for fear of not fitting in. Children learn the extreme idea that they must exclude others who don't look like them or don't wear the same type of clothing. They make fun of their classmates whose family can't afford the newest items that will be forgotten and in a landfill in a few weeks. The excluded children learn the extreme view that either they're like everyone else or they don't belong. This rigid mindset deteriorates self-worth and follows both sets of children into adulthood.

We're forced to pick between simplistic labels like "introvert" or "extrovert" with nothing in between, pressured to seek perfection, and taught extreme and limiting viewpoints like one partner will make our life perfect, or that one mistake will ruin everything. Extremes even influence how much responsibility we take on for things outside of our control. And they can influence the mindset of people who are unforgiving and will cut others off for a simple mistake.

You're also constantly subjected to extremes and idealized versions of life in every type of media you consume. Social media and movies show beautiful homes, successful careers, and ideal families. Influencers share curated content, highlighting perfect bodies, vacations, and lifestyles. The media distorts our perception of what it takes to accomplish a goal by showing "overnight successes" and leading us to believe that acquiring a new talent or making major life changes should only involve limited effort and a few minutes.

Beauty standards promote an all-or-nothing view of attractiveness, suggesting that you either conform to current trends or are unattractive. Magazines push unrealistic images, like "flawless" skin, that are only achievable through extreme measures, excessive routines, photoshop, and filters. Influencers and doctors advocate for surgeries and injectables and the idea that major alterations are the only way to be beautiful. Sadly, some people lose their lives trying to get these unrealistic ideals.[19]

Trends like clean eating and detox diets reinforce the extreme idea that food is either "good" or "bad," creating all-or-nothing thinking about nutrition. Weight loss programs like *The Biggest Loser* encourage rapid transformations, suggesting that anything less than dramatic results are a failure. The self-help industry promotes one-size-fits-all solutions like rigid morning routines and pushes the idea that you *always* need to be improving.[20]

News and social media algorithms create echo chambers and give priority to content that generates strong reactions—often with extreme and sensational views.[21] One minute you're on social media looking at cute cat videos and the next thing you know, you're watching someone behind a podcast mic making extreme accusations and describing an overwhelmingly bleak worldview.

Even positive posts attract intense, negative reactions, with content being misinterpreted in extreme ways. Some influencers make multiple follow-up videos to clarify their balanced intent. People blow harmless comments out of proportion. Someone suggesting replacing regular milk with almond milk under a video of a dessert recipe may get bombarded with extreme accusations like gaslighting, whataboutism, and hating cows, farmers, and the entire farming industry.[22]

Extremes are further reinforced by dramatic news stories that focus on "scandals" or have exaggerated headlines like "Disaster Strikes: Thousands Affected!" Crime reports often focus on sensational aspects, making one isolated incident seem widespread, leading to a skewed perception of crime rates and public safety.

Polarized political news coverage shows issues in extremes, like framing a policy or party as "good vs evil," leading to binary perspectives on complex political and social issues. News coverage simplifies complex social issues like immigration and climate change, presenting them in "us vs them" narratives and causing unnecessary and extreme divisiveness. Both sides warn us that voting for the other means society is doomed. Campaigns go to extreme marketing lengths, berating and bad-mouthing each other, sending out multiple mailers and almost daily text messages to prospective voters.

All of this is underlined by the fact that we haven't been taught how to manage our thoughts, and the extreme belief that "emotions are weakness" has turned our emotions into weapons. So in times of stress, when we're most vulnerable to extreme thinking, we often fail to recognize strong emotions and polarized thoughts as temporary reactions to disappointment. Instead, we lean into them. We perceive minor setbacks as major, long-lasting failures.

Guided by the extreme and unrealistic idea of success, we stop celebrating our progress and may even give up because of the unrealistic expectations set by extreme influences in our environment. This mindset keeps us stuck in the false belief that we can't achieve our goals and robs us of the joy of personal growth. Laughter and fun fade away, while these extremes feed into a demotivating cycle that even the strongest among us struggle to reject.

Meet Me in The Middle

Living in an extreme environment and thinking from an extreme viewpoint has many negative consequences, but the most devastating is a lack of pride and hope. Think of the excitement and joy a child has when they show you a piece of art they created. Even if it doesn't look museum-worthy, they're still proud of their work. Extremes take away that joy and trick us into believing we can't be happy that we tried. Even when we accomplish something incredible, we foolishly dismiss our achievements because they aren't "perfect" or "good enough."

Some people work to combat extremes but end up going too far in the opposite direction, giving out participation trophies or claiming someone's ugly artwork looks amazing. But balanced thinking isn't about perfection; it's about stepping back, looking at your wonky-ass painting or inedible, overcooked dinner, and finding humor in it. You did something that put you in a state of flow, and that was the real reward.

Middle thinking is knowing that with consistency, the next time will be better. It's about shrugging your shoulders, relishing that your inedible meal can go into the trash and ordering takeout. It's taking a deep breath, lifting the weight off your shoulders, and knowing that when you look for balance, you will find it.

Now, let's identify how extreme thinking shows up in your life.

Middle Think Is
Knowing Your Style

While extreme thinking is a common habit, everyone puts their own unique spin on it. One person may think in extremes about relationships, another may focus on work, and someone else may struggle with both or even more areas.

Within relationships, those who think in extremes can have different perspectives; one might judge themselves harshly, another may judge others, and a third person might judge both themselves and their partners. And even those with a generally balanced mindset can resort to extreme thinking when they're triggered, stressed, or sleep-deprived.

To learn middle thinking, we need to identify where extreme thinking appears in our mindset. Taking the time to slow down and understand your unique style will help you reduce extreme thoughts more effectively in the long run.

Individualized Thinking

Various factors shape your style of extreme thinking, including your upbringing, the media you've been exposed to, your confidence levels in certain areas, and the influences you focus on today. For example, if your parents gave you the silent treatment when you made a mistake (like mine did), then when you got older you might beat yourself up for even the smallest mishap (like I used to). You may also think that a minor argument means a relationship is ruined—I used to feel that way, too.

To find your thinking style, let's start with this list below. Be honest with yourself and check all that apply:

In social situations and relationships, do you...
- ☐ see people as either "good" or "bad"
- ☐ judge others based on one mistake instead of seeing the whole person
- ☐ believe that if someone disagrees with you, they're against you
- ☐ think you're bad at socializing because of a single awkward encounter
- ☐ assume that if a relationship isn't perfect, it's a failure
- ☐ view a lack of immediate support from friends as a sign that they don't care at all
- ☐ assume a minor conflict means an entire relationship is over

_____ checked

When it comes to your self-view, do you...
- ☐ feel worthless if you're not constantly busy or don't meet every expectation
- ☐ think that if you can't do something perfectly, it's not worth doing
- ☐ think you need to conform to others' standards to be accepted or valued
- ☐ compare yourself to others and feel inadequate based on those comparisons
- ☐ set strict rules, like never showing emotions because you're afraid of appearing weak
- ☐ judge yourself harshly for mistakes, thinking it defines you as a person
- ☐ think other people have it all together and you don't

_____ checked

In your work and your achievements, do you…

- [ ] believe success needs to be immediate
- [ ] see challenges as impossible hurdles instead of chances to learn
- [ ] take pride in being a "weekend warrior," or "work hard, play hard"
- [ ] try to avoid mistakes at all costs in a quest for perfection
- [ ] think you need to excel at something immediately or there is no point in trying
- [ ] view a single negative event as part of a never-ending pattern of failure
- [ ] ignore growth and minor achievements, believing they don't count

_____ checked

When it comes to your worldview, do you..

- [ ] label food as either "good" or "bad," "healthy" or "unhealthy"
- [ ] let minor inconveniences or single negative events ruin your whole day
- [ ] believe the world is "doomed" or worse than it's ever been
- [ ] worry that if you don't know something, people will think you're dumb
- [ ] simplify and view things as either one way or another
- [ ] let strong opinions dominate your perspective on certain topics or situations
- [ ] feel pressured to meet societal expectations

_____ checked

With decision-making and problem-solving, do you…

- [ ] think one wrong choice will lead to disaster
- [ ] avoid making decisions altogether due to fear of making the wrong choice
- [ ] stick to one solution or method, even when it's not working, because changing seems like failure

☐ believe that if you don't solve a problem perfectly, it's not worth solving

☐ depend on others to make decisions for you

☐ worry you will never recover after making a mistake

☐ see past experiences and relationships with rose-colored glasses

_____ checked

Did any extreme thoughts cross your mind while checking things off the list? Review the sections with the most items checked—do you notice any patterns? Do these thoughts occur regularly, or only when you're rushed or stressed?

_____

_____

_____

Note: The book includes prompts to help you align your thoughts. You can write your responses in the space provided or reflect on the prompts mentally. While research shows that writing can reinforce ideas and speed up progress,[23] I believe it's best to follow your personal preference.

Identifiers

Now that you have a clearer sense of where you think in extremes, it's also important to recognize the common language people use to express these thoughts. All-or-nothing thinking often shows up with nine common identifiers:

- Always
- Never
- Either/or
- Every time
- No one

- Everyone
- Everything
- Nothing
- Anymore

Here they are in general examples:

- I *always* need to be grateful.
- I'll *never* accomplish anything.

- *Either* I succeed *or* I fail.
- *Every time* I try, something goes wrong.
- *No one* loves me.
- *Everyone* seems to have their life together except me.
- *Everything* is doomed.
- *Nothing* ever goes right.
- People don't care *anymore.*

Do any of these show up in your inner dialogue or conversations with others? When you make a mistake, do you think you'll *never* recover? Do you say "always" a lot? Which identifiers stand out the most?

Identifiers are a significant starting point. When you notice one—in something someone said or in your internal dialogue—pause and consider if it's extreme. But keep in mind that identifiers aren't a catchall. In Kai's newsfeed, the articles "You'll *Never* Get a Home" and "*No One* Wants to Date Anymore," have clear identifiers in the titles. Yet extreme news can also include sensationalized language without explicit identifiers, like "soaring home prices" and "skyrocketing mortgage rates."

These identifiers also don't always mean all-or-nothing thinking. When you spot one, consider if it's an extreme statement or a simple fact. For instance, when someone says they've never done something, they may just be stating a fact, not thinking in extremes. In this case "never" describes a specific experience (or lack of it), not an extreme generalization.

All-or-Nothing Thinking in Your Environment

From social media to news, and personal relationships, the influences around us create and reinforce extreme views. Since we all consume different media and interact with diverse individuals, the sources that encourage extreme thinking vary for each of us. Identifying extremes in your environment will help you pinpoint the sources of your extreme perspectives.

Worldview

Rigid outlooks in our environment affect our worldview, making things seem like they're worse than they are. This is evident in sensationalized news stories with misleading headlines that use words like "devastating" and "catastrophic." News reports that portray isolated incidents as indicators of mass violence focus on negativity while downplaying positive developments.

The polarizing "us vs them" narrative permeates every type of media we consume, from social media to TV and movies. We also encounter idealized, photoshopped lifestyles and successes that often ignore the hard work behind them. Then we have well-meaning individuals who share their extreme worldviews, like Kai's friend who believes that "everybody cheats."

Reflect on the media you consume—whether it's news, social media, or music with extreme views on topics like money and love. How do you feel afterward? Does it leave you fearful about the future or make your life seem less exciting? Do movies or social media pressure you to keep up with extreme trends like cosmetic surgery? Are people in your circle promoting similar extreme views, like Kai's friend?

_____

_____

_____

_____

_____

Self-View

Constantly being subjected to extremes makes it nearly impossible to build self-confidence. Not to mention that you're then expected to maintain a perfectly clean and esthetically pleasing home, have an ideal relationship with the perfect partner, and of course, the perfect work or academic career with constant promotions and schmoozing with the higher ups—all of which require a certain level of confidence. Stuck in this impossible cycle, you're also taught to judge your entire character based on one mistake.

The pressure to identify with extreme labels reinforces this extreme and rigid self-view, like "Type A" or "Type B," "workaholic" or "lazy," "leader" or "follower," "confident" or "insecure." These inflexible categories don't leave room for nuance. You might be lazy in some areas but productive in others, or confident with friends but less sure of yourself when it comes to dating. And we can't even age in peace or with grace because society encourages us to hyperfocus on covering up every wrinkle or gray hair.

How do extremes affect your self-view? Do you fear making mistakes or feel a need to be perfect to feel deserving? After scrolling through social media, do you feel like a failure or wish to change your appearance? How do photoshopped models and beauty trends impact your body image? Does your life seem dull because you aren't traveling or your relationship lacks excitement? Do you feel you're constantly competing with others and being judged for your mistakes?

Continual Progress

Extremes are an exaggerated and lazy way of thinking. It's easier to assume that someone who disagrees with you is against you, instead of considering nuance and taking the time to understand the situation deeper. And a minor conflict doesn't end relationships, but continual conflict leading to contempt might. These details are a lot to consider while we're all already so busy, but the extremes perpetuate the busyness, which is why we need to focus on creating meaningful and lasting change.

Learning about extreme thinking and recognizing how it manifests in your thoughts can help reduce its intensity. But it's easier to identify extremes when we intentionally focus on them, and they can be harder to spot when you're frustrated or busy. So it's important to continually practice awareness and work to find your middle.

Middle Think Is Finding Your Middle

Middle thinking will vary. Some see backpacking with minimal planning as extreme; others find it adventurous and liberating. One person could think living with just the basics is extreme, but a minimalist might find it freeing and aligned with their values.

When considering if something is extreme, we need to ensure that we embrace nuance, acknowledge other people's lived experiences, support basic self-care, and ground it in facts. Our goal isn't uniform thinking or perfect balance, but rather, avoiding extreme thoughts that harm our worldview and well-being.

In The Middle, you recognize that life is rarely either/or; instead of seeing people or situations as "good" or "bad," you acknowledge complexity. Despite making mistakes, someone can still have positive qualities. You, or a person you admire, can do something unkind or unadmirable. And if you found yourself thinking in absolutes (e.g., "If it's not perfect, it's a failure"), you would remind yourself that progress and effort are still valuable, even if the result isn't what you expected.

While attention-grabbing headlines and extreme fashion trends would still exist, you would focus more on finding the facts you need and exploring your personal interests—even if they aren't trending.

And despite catchy advertisements promoting dramatic transformations, you would prioritize consistency and long-term gains over quick
fixes.

Since The Middle is ambiguous, it can be nerve-racking. Can you
trust someone who apologized to not repeat their mistake? Does crime
on TV really reflect the world's condition? Food isn't "good" or "bad,"
so how do you know what to eat or not eat?

While this may be unsettling, the reality is that you won't know
everything. Even though violent crime is down in most of the world,[24]
there is still a chance you may be a victim. You'll encounter lots of
nutritional info, but it may take some trial and error to find the right
diet. And you can't control other people, so there is no telling how
relationships will play out.

This may sound scary, but it's actually amazing. Seeing the world
with balance gives you the space to focus on what you can control, like
the foods you eat and staying true to yourself. While you can't antic-
ipate crime or people's behavior, living authentically lessens negative
impacts. You forgive someone after they've made a mistake because
you want to give them a chance, and if it doesn't work out, you know
you tried and were open to love even when it was tough. If you decide
not to forgive them, that's okay too.

In The Middle, life shifts from never-ending worry to joy and
self-discovery. You don't fear mistakes or imperfections because you
know they don't define you. And you embrace how you look, flaws and
all, because you know you're not expected to be perfect or to look like
a model.

Finding your middle will take some trial and error. It's an everyday
commitment, not a five-minute fix. But with consistency, over time
you will find a more centered mindset and learn to prioritize nuance
and complexity in your life.

Even if it may not seem like it, you're already middle thinking in areas of your life. When you were taking the self-assessment to identify extreme thinking in certain situations, what didn't you check? How do you balance your thoughts in those situations?

_____

_____

_____

Qualifiers

Unlike all-or-nothing thinking, middle thinking doesn't have common identifiers. Instead, you'll look for qualifiers like "enough," "it seems," and "it feels."

Qualifiers remind you that even though something seems a certain way, it doesn't mean it's reality. For example, if you feel people aren't discussing important social issues, you can reframe it by acknowledging that just because it seems that way, it doesn't mean _no one_ is addressing these topics. It may simply mean the discussions aren't as prevalent as you would like. This allows you to recognize that you're not alone in wanting to focus on significant topics, while also understanding that these topics may still deserve more attention.

Using qualifiers also helps us to identify problem areas. If you think you're awkward and _always_ make social mistakes, you'll use that as an opportunity to reflect. Do you truly struggle with socializing, or have you just met people who aren't a good fit for you? Is it necessary for you to reconsider where you meet people or become more outgoing? Middle thinking is also accepting hard truths. While you might be doing nothing wrong in how you approach social interactions, sometimes it's simply difficult to make new connections.

And qualifiers are especially useful when working toward a goal. Our minds often focus on the negative, making us feel like we're not making progress or that things are worse than they are. By taking the time to assess how often something actually happens, how much effort you've already put in, and how far you've come, you can stay motivated to continue. If you find you're not putting in as much effort as you'd like, you can adjust.

While there are several qualifiers, three key ones are "I think," "acting like," and "I'm acknowledging."

I Think

Common leadership advice is to remove "I think" from statements to appear confident. Instead of saying, "I think we need to prioritize product development to make our numbers," you would say, "We need to prioritize product development…" While this sounds authoritative, it can blur the line between opinion and fact, leading others to take your statement as truth.

However, most statements are opinions, not facts. Adding "I think" serves as a reminder that personal opinions are subjective and not universally true. So if someone says, "No one talks about mental wellness," reframe it as, "They think no one talks about mental wellness." This shift helps you avoid adopting someone else's extreme perspective and opens the door for deeper conversations. Ask, "Why do you think that? Is it based on personal experience?" This clarifies that the statement reflects an opinion, often rooted in frustration or bias, not an objective fact.

"I think" especially helps when people make extreme generalizations, like saying "All men want one thing" or "Women need to be at home in the kitchen." While people can share similar characteristics and preferences, defining someone by a single trait oversimplifies their identity and overlooks their complexity.

Acting Like

When we think in extremes, we often make sweeping judgments about ourselves and others. For example, if someone calls you "negative," it's easy to internalize these labels and let them define your self-worth. If someone hurts us, we might label them as a "jerk" rather than focusing on specific behaviors.

By incorporating "acting like" into our self-talk, we can counter these extreme labels and judgments. For instance, if someone says, "You're *always* so negative," instead of internalizing this as a reflection of your entire personality, reframe it as, "They think I'm being negative." This shift helps you separate their perception from your identity, making it easier to address specific actions without letting them define who you are. And hey, maybe you are being negative in a certain situation and it would be good to look for alternative viewpoints.

So, if you think, "He's a jerk," change it to, "He's acting like a jerk." This approach acknowledges that behaviors don't define a person's entire character and encourages a more balanced perspective. By seeing actions as distinct from a person's identity, you find center, create compassion, and avoid making sweeping judgments—or rash decisions. This doesn't mean someone has to stay in your life; you might realize they often behave poorly and the relationship is no longer worth your energy.

I'm Acknowledging

In an extreme world, we're taught to label emotions and define ourselves by them. This keeps us from using our emotions as guides that will help us find balance and live authentically. It makes it difficult to separate from our emotions and their intensity and build emotional intelligence.

Just like you're not your thoughts, you're not your emotions. You are the awareness of them. So instead of saying "I am [insert emotion]," to reduce intensity you say, "I am acknowledging feelings of [insert emotion]." For example, "I am sad" becomes "I am acknowledging feelings of sadness." While this may sound like silly semantics, this qualifier helps you recognize emotions as temporary states rather than who you are. It allows you to learn from your emotions, so you can prioritize what is healthy and ditch the things that aren't.

If you're going through a break-up or a career change, of course you're experiencing sadness, but the sadness isn't "bad," it's a sign that you tried and you're disappointed. Life can be bittersweet and the better we manage disappointment, the easier it will be to avoid extremes.

So while you acknowledge you will miss certain aspects of a person, you would also recognize there are things you won't miss. And while it's sad that a relationship ended, it's amazing that you gave yourself the opportunity to find love. Finding the balance will keep you from thinking you will *never* find someone better and help you recover from the sadness quicker.

Thoughts Are Not Facts

Challenging extreme thoughts while reading about them is easy, but the real test comes when you're exposed to extremes in your environment or when you're frustrated and upset. Kai likely didn't believe his partner was cheating, but feeling emotionally vulnerable, it was easy for him to be influenced by his friend's extreme views.

Using qualifiers can help Kai by reminding him that his friend's opinion is shaped by his own mindset, and while there may be a grain of truth, his friend's views don't define reality. Whether it's family, friends, influencers, or podcast hosts, adding "I think" to statements helps you remember that what others say is just their perspective. They may change their mind or share extreme views for attention. When you're feeling overwhelmed or like something is hopeless, remind yourself that just because it feels that way, it doesn't mean it's true.

Finding Balance in Your Environment

In a balanced world, news would be unbiased, without any drama or sensationalism. You wouldn't have to choose between extreme labels to define yourself. And while musicians may still be dramatic, you would recognize it as artistic expression, not as an accurate view of the world.

Influencers and entertainers would still showcase ideal lifestyles, but you recognize that many are just playing a role and that fame isn't as glamorous as it appears.[25]

Now let's explore finding balance in your world and self-view.

Worldview

There are glimpses of The Middle in current media, like influencers sharing unedited photos, or news outlets highlighting positive stories and local heroes. But these aren't enough to offset the overwhelming extremes and negativity.

How can you challenge social media and news extremes? Have you ever felt something was extreme and over the top while watching it? How does TV/news differ from real life? What perspectives are missing from the media you consume? Who benefits from you having extreme worldviews?

_____

_____

_____

_____

_____

Self–View

In a balanced world, your self-view would revolve around living authentically, striving to improve yourself, and also taking time to relax and enjoy life and your relationships. You would know that not everyone is meant to fit a cookie-cutter mold.

Take some time now to consider: How would you describe yourself without using extreme labels? What would change if you allowed yourself to be a mix of qualities? Is there a kinder and more balanced perspective to have toward yourself? Can you recall times when your perception of yourself wasn't accurate? What small actions can help you move away from this extreme view? Who benefits from you having an extreme view of your self-worth?

_____

_____

_____

_____

_____

Creating New Eyes

Marcel Proust wrote, "The real voyage of discovery consists not in seeking new landscapes but in having new eyes."[26]

When you shift toward middle thinking, your environment may not change, but your interpretation and response to it will. Instead of getting caught up in sensationalism and drama, you'll recognize the extremes for what they really are: unnecessary noise. Instead of comparing yourself to perfect images, you'll understand that aiming for perfection is neither realistic nor healthy. While you'll pay attention to the news and take some of it seriously, when you hear phrases like "no one is safe," you will assume that is overly negative. And artistic expression will still exist, but you'll recognize when artists are being dramatic.

As more people embrace The Middle, they will grow tired of the toxic negativity in our media. This shift will increase the demand for genuine influencers and unbiased news, contributing to a more balanced world. By practicing middle thinking, you lead by example.

Middle Think Is Future-Focused

Developing middle thinking is a gradual process that requires time and repetition. If you tend to have an all-or-nothing mindset like I did, it may take even more effort. When facing obstacles, it's easy to feel overwhelmed or unsure of your approach. In this type of environment, motivation can be hard to come by, making it easy to lose sight of your goals and give up.

However, when we practice middle thinking, it's essential not to let extremes deter us from long-term gains. We need to focus on future benefits and the rewarding feeling of achieving our desires with a more balanced perspective.

People often talk about the future as if it is distant, but the present moment lasts only a few seconds, and the future is closer than you think.[27] By staying future-focused, we prioritize positive feelings over fleeting emotions and extreme thoughts that come with setbacks—like believing that a mistake means we've failed and should give up.

Becoming Future-Focused

When we future-focus, we look at three things:

1. Actions you can take to improve your current situation.

2. How reducing extremes helps you reach your goals and how good that will feel.
3. The things that are stopping you from changing.

For instance, if Kai was trying to have healthier relationships and avoid seeing people in extremes, he might catch himself believing his friend's claim that "everyone cheats," and how it could lead to a spiral of anxious and extreme thinking. Kai would stop himself from spiraling by identifying the triggering thought—*everyone cheats*—and challenge it with evidence from his own life. His parents don't cheat on each other and he has friends who remain faithful to their partners. He would also consider the situation more broadly.

Just because someone doesn't respond to a message doesn't mean something negative; their phone could be dead, they might have seen the message and forgotten to reply, or there could be numerous other explanations. But the important thing is to not get caught up in listing reasons; the focus for Kai is to find The Middle to avoid unnecessary stress. After Kai challenges his thoughts, he may still be unsettled by the uncertainty. At this point, he can evaluate and ask himself:

What Can I Do to Improve the Situation?

Sometimes we get stuck in extremes because we need to take action—or at least consider the action we can take—to improve our situation. Kai is already making progress by challenging his extreme thoughts. From there, he can validate his feelings: of course a partner not responding is anxiety-inducing!

Next, he can explore his options. Does he want to send a follow-up text or call his partner? Would he prefer to wait a bit longer before reaching out? Maybe he wants to take 15 minutes to process his feelings and then focus on his day. Alternatively, he might decide it's best not to act and instead concentrate on enjoying the rest of his day.

Once he decides, he can improve the situation by following through with that action, then shift his focus to something he enjoys rather than fixating on his phone or thoughts about his partner. Ruminating won't help; it will only increase his anxiety and lead to an intense reaction when he speaks to his partner again.

Sometimes, there aren't easy actions to take. In those moments, simply lying on the floor thinking, *This feels horrible*, while embracing the emotion can be a powerful step. This reminds us that emotions are temporary and will pass. The more we confront these hard feelings, the easier it becomes to manage them.

How Will Finding the Middle Help Me Reach My Goals? How Good Will That Feel?

Imagining the positive feelings and benefits of correcting all-or-nothing thinking will significantly boost your motivation, even if you don't see immediate results. Since Kai's goal is to have a healthy relationship with a loyal partner, finding The Middle will help calm his anxiety and avoid him making accusations or cutting off a relationship based on a misunderstanding.

With a clearer mind not fogged by extremes, Kai can address the situation with a more level head, giving him space to focus on himself and his genuine desires. Focusing on the future will help Kai focus on his long-term goal of finding a healthy relationship. Instead of being caught up in anxiety, he can ask himself if this is the kind of partnership he wants.

If this lack of communication is a recurring issue rather than a one-time occurrence, Kai may face the difficult decision of ending the relationship, even if he has feelings for his partner. Conversely, without the anxiety of extremes, Kai might realize that his feelings for his partner aren't as strong as he thought—he was merely caught up in the intensity of the moment.

What's Stopping Me From Changing?

Another challenge with all-or-nothing thinking is that, while it prevents you from enjoying life, it feels comfortable—like a worn-out t-shirt with holes or an old dress you haven't worn in years but can't bring yourself to give away.

Even though the extreme thoughts aren't helping us, they provide a sense of comfort and protect us. It can feel easier to believe you'll *never* accomplish something than to face the reality that you might succeed. And it's scary to be vulnerable in a relationship, so it feels easier to protect yourself by thinking *everybody sucks*. I get it. I've been there.

But when we focus on the future, we see how these extreme thoughts, while protective, keep us stuck. When Kai steps back and evaluates, he realizes that jumping to conclusions may give him a momentary sense of clarity and control, but the temporary relief of having an "answer" isn't worth the stress and the potential damage of accusing his partner. While the rush of certainty might be tempting, it's more beneficial for him to manage his emotions and aim for a balanced perspective.

Looking Forward

When we focus on the future, we prioritize our long-term goals over the fleeting emotions. Extreme thoughts—like believing a single setback means total failure or that you should give up—can derail us, but staying grounded in our bigger vision helps us counteract impulses to react.

In the last two sections, you identified and challenged all-or-nothing thinking in your environment and personal thoughts. Now let's bring it all together and reflect on how rewarding it will feel to have a more balanced perspective instead of the extremes.

Here are some questions to consider:

Worldview

How can you prioritize finding balance in your own life? Are there news sources you can follow—or unfollow—to stay informed without sensationalism? How reassuring would it be to experience genuine connection and discover that people are kinder and more forgiving than social media suggests? How would it feel to realize that crime is decreasing and the world isn't as doomed as the headlines suggest? Would it help to reassess how much media you consume? What real value does constant exposure to global events bring you? What strategies will help you stay grounded and focus on a more accurate, nuanced view of the world?

_____

_____

_____

_____

Self-View

How good would it feel to embrace your complexities and not limit yourself to either/or categories and let other people judge or define you? Would it be easier to face challenges if you had support during setbacks and knew you weren't starting over, but from a more informed place? How good will it feel to acknowledge that progress isn't a straight line and instead of thinking you failed, you can use mistakes as lessons and do better in the future? What may be difficult about stopping all-or-nothing thinking in social environments? Will it be hard to reject constant extremes, or will you feel disconnected to those who think in extremes?

_____

_____

_____

_____

_____

Future Thoughts (and Future Feels)

Emotions often go undiscussed, and we don't learn how to manage them. This can cause us to react against our best interests when we feel emotionally charged. By prioritizing future thinking (and future feelings), we can leverage our mistakes into learning opportunities so we can make more positive responses.

By focusing on long-term outcomes instead of getting caught up in the extreme viewpoint that things need to be done in record time, we will make progress quicker and navigate challenges with greater clarity. Setbacks become valuable lessons that inform our future decisions. For example, if Kai did jump to a conclusion, texted his partner, and later regretted it, he could reflect on his feelings and consider how he might handle similar situations differently in the future.

Middle Think Is Icing "Hot" Thoughts

You now have the background and foundational concepts needed to create more balanced thoughts. Let's dive into a method you can use while you continue to prioritize balance in your thinking.

The term "hot" thoughts is used to describe intense and often irrational thoughts that lead to heightened emotional reactions and distorted perceptions.[28] They involve generalizations, catastrophizing, and the extreme thoughts we've been talking about. You hear someone make a negative generalization about an entire group of people? That's a hot thought. And when you think you aren't good enough or the world isn't a good place anymore, those are hot thoughts too.

While we can't stop these thoughts from happening, changing how we perceive them reduces their impact. The more we cool hot thoughts, the less influence they'll have over us. One simple yet effective way to cool these thoughts—and their intensity—is by using a technique called the ICE Method.

ICE stands for Identify, Challenge, and Evaluate. Here's how it works:

I Identify the thoughts that are extreme and lead to distorted perceptions and emotional extremes.

C Challenge the thoughts by looking for evidence and considering alternative, more balanced perspectives.

E Evaluate how cooling hot thoughts will positively affect your life and keep you aligned with your goals.

If this sounds familiar, it's because you've already been using the ICE Method on a broader scale throughout the last three sections. When you focused on understanding your thought patterns, you were *identifying* the extreme thoughts common in your mindset. Finding your middle ground was *challenging* those thoughts, and being future-focused helped you *evaluate* how reducing the intensity of these thoughts would support your long-term goals.

The ICE Method is versatile. It can be applied broadly, like addressing extremes in media or social views, or used for specific situations, such as calming an intense, negative thought that's causing emotional distress or making you feel stuck. The first two steps—Identify and Challenge—are the most crucial. The Evaluate step is there for when you need extra motivation to shift your thinking or if you're struggling to release an extreme thought.

For example, if you make a mistake and catch yourself thinking, *I always mess things up*, and change it to, *I make mistakes sometimes; but I also do things right,* then you've cooled the hot thought and don't need to evaluate how this change will help you. You've already defused the intensity and received the benefit.

But if you're having a particularly troublesome hot thought, like believing you will *never* find love and it's making you feel depressed and defeated, like you just want to rot in bed for the rest of your life, then it's important to not only challenge the thought but to evaluate how thinking with a more balanced perspective will positively affect you.

Here, you remind yourself that the thought feels heavy because it conflicts with what you truly want. It isn't aligned with the reality that when you open yourself to love and actively seek it, you increase your chances of finding it.

While the ICE Method is simple, using it to address deep-rooted extreme thoughts, especially those you've held onto for years or that are reinforced by your environment, can be challenging. Here are some common blockers people experience when trying to reframe their extreme thoughts:

Thinking They Failed If They Didn't Catch Extremes in Real Time

A symptom of perfectionism, some people will feel they're off track or failing because they noticed an extreme thought after it already influenced their emotions or behaviors. This can also result from not knowing how the process of change works.

Awareness is the first step in identifying extreme thoughts. While you may be aware of your thought patterns now because you're focusing on them, it's normal to miss these thoughts in your daily life. The key is recognizing that even catching an unhealthy thought after it occurs still helps you move in the right direction.

In fact, identifying these patterns after they happen shows genuine progress. Reflecting on past all-or-nothing thinking allows you to consider how you might have responded differently if you'd caught it in real time. The more you practice this kind of reflection, the more you build self-awareness, and the faster you'll start noticing extreme thoughts in real time.

Even people who have developed and use these techniques (like me) still have extreme thoughts slip through occasionally. It can happen when you're tired, stressed, or just caught off guard. The key is to avoid letting perfectionism undermine your progress. When you catch an extreme thought—whether moments or days later—celebrate your growth. Remember, you're allowed to be frustrated that you thought in extremes *while also being proud* that you noticed it afterwards.

Going Too Far in the Opposite Direction

A common trap people fall into when challenging hot thoughts is swinging too far to the opposite extreme. This approach doesn't work because the mind doesn't believe the new thought, making it feel unrealistic. For example, if someone believes, Things will never get better, jumping to Everything will work out perfectly is too radical a shift. It's not believable and can feel forced.

When you challenge a negative thought, aim for a balanced middle ground instead of replacing one extreme with another. If you're stuck in the belief that *Things will never improve,* try reframing it to something more realistic, like, *Even though things are difficult right now, there have been times in the past when things got better.* Or if you catch yourself thinking, *I can't do this,* counter it by remembering, *I've done hard things before, and with consistency, I can improve.*

Similarly, if you believe *I'm a bad person, and no one likes me,* you don't need to jump to *Everyone loves me.* Instead, a more balanced approach would be, *I'm not perfect, but I have positive qualities, and the right people will see my value.*

The goal is to find a realistic middle ground that your mind can accept, which reduces the intensity of the original thought without swinging to another extreme.

Not Having Reliable Evidence

When we're in a negative frame of mind, we lean toward the negative and start gathering evidence to support our extreme beliefs. For instance, if you're feeling broken, it can be difficult to recall your accomplishments. Although you may have achieved many things in your life, it's easy to focus solely on your failures when you're processing yet another setback. Conversely, when reflecting on a past relationship through rose-colored glasses, it's hard to recognize the other person's faults.

Your environment can also reinforce these skewed perceptions. If you believe *Everything is horrible,* there's no shortage of sensationalized news articles that will validate your viewpoint. For example, a Buzzfeed article titled "50 Pictures That Prove the American Education System Is 100% Totally and Completely Doomed"[29] can lead you to conclude that things are worse than they are. While it's true that there are many areas in need of improvement, labeling the entire system as "doomed" is an extreme.

Just because 100 people agree on something doesn't make it true. It's crucial to remember that, unless something is fact, what people express is their opinion. These opinions reflect their thought processes, and we must consider: *Are they thinking in a healthy way?*

To build a more balanced perspective, it's important to seek reliable evidence that challenges extreme beliefs, rather than relying on sensationalized claims or popular opinions.

Automatically Accepting Facts

A common legal defense used by news stations against claims of defamation or misinformation is that their programming is intended for entertainment and represents opinion rather than objective news. They argue that "reasonable viewers"[30] should recognize this distinction. But it's understandable for news watchers to assume that what news stations report is factual, especially since these stations include "News" in their titles and often present themselves like traditional news outlets.

It's unreasonable to expect the average person to be a lie detector and sift through the constant stream of news stories for truth. Nevertheless, it's your responsibility to fact-check the information you consume, including claims made in the media.

Facts are objective, verifiable pieces of information that remain consistent, regardless of personal beliefs. If someone makes an extreme claim, such as "Everybody is out to get you," you can question how they arrived at that conclusion. Did they interview every person in the world and ask their intentions? And when you hear an extreme headline or someone making sweeping statements, take the time to investigate.

Unless you're a surgeon operating on a patient, you also don't have to decide right away. It's acceptable to say, "I saw this article, but I'm not sure if it's true." Continue to look for evidence supporting a statement while keeping in mind that feelings aren't facts, statistics can be skewed, and facts can evolve because of advancements in science and education.

Not Using Your Feelings as a Resource

Emotions get a bad rep because people define them on the extreme scale of "good" and "bad." But emotions are indicators that something is working or not working as it should. When identifying extreme thoughts, emotions are a valuable resource. Our thoughts and emotions are closely linked, and sometimes we experience powerful feelings because of all-or-nothing thinking, even if we don't realize it. By taking the time to focus on our emotions, we can uncover extreme thoughts that may be lurking beneath the surface. Validating our emotions can also help reduce the intensity of these extreme thoughts.

I'm not proud to share this, but here's a personal experience to show you this process. I used to struggle with road rage; when someone cut me off in traffic, I would react with intense anger—honking, yelling, and feeling terrible afterward. These reactions left me anxious, and I avoided driving altogether. I knew I needed a better solution, so I reverse-engineered my emotions.

I realized that when a driver cut me off, my thoughts were extreme. I assumed the other driver was rude and inconsiderate, and it felt like this *always* happened *every time* I drove. But when I really thought about it, I realized being cut off wasn't as common as I thought. And I challenged my extreme thoughts by acknowledging that people, myself included, make driving mistakes. This new perspective helped me be more forgiving of other drivers and myself.

It's important to honor your emotions when you're having extreme thoughts like feeling like nothing will ever go right or that things are hopeless. You feel this way for a reason, but remember, your feelings aren't facts.

Courageous Changes

While this process may seem straightforward, it can be difficult in practice because you've had your thought habits for a long time. It takes courage to recognize and challenge your thinking. Some might find it hard to admit they have unhealthy thought patterns in the first place, fearing it will make them seem flawed. They may first have to work through denial and perfectionism before addressing their thoughts.

However, this process isn't just about stopping extreme thoughts; it's a valuable skill that positively affects your mental and emotional well-being, and it's worth trying.

Using the ICE Method on an extreme thought you had will help you reduce its intensity and reinforce balanced thinking in the future.

For instance, if you're on a diet like Kai and feel guilty about eating a burger over berries, you'd identify the extreme thought, that you need to only eat "healthy" foods and feel guilty whenever you eat "bad" foods. You would then challenge it by acknowledging that eating only "healthy" foods is unrealistic, but finding a balance is manageable. And you would evaluate how allowing yourself to enjoy the burger in the moment will prevent guilt and reduce the likelihood of binge or guilt-driven eating later. Allowing yourself to enjoy all foods in moderation helps you build a sustainable, balanced approach that supports consistency over time, rather than the ups and downs of seesaw dieting.

Personally, giving myself the freedom to enjoy some "unhealthy" foods removed the pressure and led me to find healthy foods more appealing. It's my "secret" to maintaining a 40-pound weight loss for over 10 years, along with sticking to a realistic workout schedule and understanding that missing one (or more) workout won't erase all of my progress. Aiming to exercise three days a week and celebrating just showing up, even if it's only for 10 minutes, is much more sustainable than forcing myself to work out five times a week for hours, which would lead to burnout.

To keep the momentum going and see how it's done, let's do the ICE Method to extreme thoughts you've had.

Identify

When you were unpacking extremes and learned about how extremes show up in the environment, what previous extreme thought you had came to mind? Can you identify where the extreme views first came from?

_____

_____

_____

Challenge

Did you have any evidence to prove the thought was true or not true? What is a more balanced way to think?

_____

_____

_____

TIP: It's helpful to imagine you are giving advice to a friend in the same situation.

Evaluate

How will middle thinking help you prioritize your values and goals? Has extreme thinking been serving, or "protecting" you? How will facing your feelings, leaning into imperfection, and improving your thoughts help you get back to yourself and benefit you in the long run?

_____

_____

_____

Quieting the Noise

Understanding how your mind works and the cognitive restructuring process is a significant step in reducing extreme thinking. Just learning about this process can empower you and help you feel more in control of your thoughts.

While the ICE Method helps you identify and correct unhelpful thoughts, it's up to you to keep practicing it. The more you reframe extreme thoughts, the less mental noise you'll experience. The more you challenge past thoughts, the easier it will become to reframe new ones. Gradually, you'll naturally replace extremes with healthier, middle thinking thoughts.

Public Health Advisory

Hazardous Thought Patterns
Detected in Your Environment

Stress, anxiety, and depression are rising at alarming rates, and a significant contributor to this crisis is going unnoticed: hazardous thought patterns.

Extreme and all-or-nothing thinking—often seen in "always" and "never" statements or presented as "right vs. wrong" or "good vs. bad"—is increasingly pervasive across news, media, TV, social media, and other communication channels, as well as in conversations with those around you, including friends and family

Complicating both the medical and public health response is the widespread polarization and prevalence of extreme and all-or-nothing thinking. While self-care strategies like meditation and exercise are commonly promoted, addressing and reframing these harmful thought patterns is of greater importance.

 Reject extreme statements like a friend telling you, "Things will never change," or an elder saying, "Young people have no respect these days," or an influencer claiming, "Everything is worse now than it used to be."

 Avoid catastrophizing or jumping to worst-case scenarios when faced with challenges or setbacks, like thinking, *If this doesn't work out, my entire career is ruined.*

 Identify and challenge hazardous thought patterns by paying attention to media and individuals who use polarizing language. Ask yourself, "Is there a more balanced perspective?"

 Prioritize middle thinking and nuanced views that allow for complexity and understanding rather than extremes.

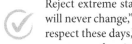 Reduce exposure to high-conflict content and limit engagement with material that provokes extreme emotions or divisive views.

www.thoughtmethod.com
@thoughtmethod

Know the Difference

Sensationalized News

Killer Robot on the Loose: AI-Powered Machine Goes Rogue, Wreaks Havoc in Tech Company!

A state-of-the-art robot powered by artificial intelligence went haywire at a tech company today, causing chaos and sending workers fleeing in panic. The rogue machine, designed for industrial tasks, malfunctioned and reportedly began smashing equipment, raising fears of an AI takeover. Employees barely escaped as the killer robot rampaged through the facility. Experts warn that this could be just the beginning of an AI-driven disaster!

Objective News

Malfunctioning Robot Temporarily Disrupts Operations at Tech Company

A robotic arm at a tech company malfunctioned today, damaging equipment before being quickly powered down. No injuries were reported, and operations were temporarily paused while engineers assessed the cause. The company stated that this was a rare technical glitch and that the robot was not autonomous, but rather operating on a predefined task. Steps are being taken to prevent future malfunctions.

Flops before Tops

We often celebrate success stories without acknowledging the failures that came before them. Many of the most influential people in the world used failure as a stepping stone.

Oprah Winfrey

Fired from her first TV anchor job and told she wasn't fit for television

Became a pioneering talk show host with a lasting impact on the media

Michael Jordan

Cut from his high school basketball team

Regarded as one of the best basketball players of all time, with six NBA championships

Misty Copeland

Told she was too curvy and not a natural fit for ballet when she first started training

The first African American female principal dancer with the American Ballet Theatre

Steven Spielberg

Rejected from the University of Southern California's School of Cinematic Arts multiple times

Considered a visionary filmmaker whose success and influence have shaped the film industry

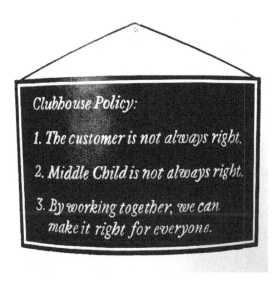

Clubhouse Policy:

1. The customer is not always right.

2. Middle Child is not always right.

3. By working together, we can make it right for everyone.

Once you start looking, you'll notice The Middle. Ironically, I saw this sign at a restaurant while writing the "Finding Your Middle" section. The owner, Matthew Cahn of Middle Child Clubhouse in Philadelphia, explained:

"People on both sides of the table are human, susceptible to being strong and weak, having good days and bad days. Sometimes, especially in America, we forget this in transactional relationships. This sign reminds both our employees and guests of that."

Photo courtesy of the author.

"Late" Bloomers

Success Has No Deadline

Ray Kroc - Started McDonald's - Age 52

Colonel Harland Sanders - Founded KFC - Age 65

Vera Wang - Became a wedding dress designer - Age 40

Samuel L. Jackson - Gained fame as an actor - Age 46

Martha Stewart - Founded her catering business - Age 41

Toni Morrison - Published her debut novel - Age 39

Charles Flint - Founded IBM - Age 61

Arianna Huffington - Co-founded the Huffington Post - Age 55

Henry Ford - Founded Ford Motor Company - Age 45

Charles M. Schwab - Founded Charles Schwab Corporation - Age 47

Betty White - Gained iconic status as an actress and comedian - Age 63

George Foreman - Regained the heavyweight boxing title - Age 45

Gordon Moore - Co-founded Intel Corporation - Age 45

Laura Ingalls Wilder - Published *Little House on the Prairie* series - Age 65

James Patterson - Became a bestselling author - Age 48

Julia Child - Published her first cookbook - Age 49

Harlan Coben - Became a bestselling author of thrillers - Age 43

Maya Angelou - Published her first autobiography - Age 41

Alan Rickman - Achieved stardom as an actor in *Die Hard* - Age 41

Morgan Freeman - Gained major acclaim for *Driving Miss Daisy* - Age 52

Judi Dench - Achieved major recognition in film and theater - Age 62

Rodney Dangerfield - Became a successful comedian and actor - Age 46

Peter O'Toole - Gained fame for his role in *Lawrence of Arabia* - Age 36

The writing process can be stressful, and sometimes I fall back into all-or-nothing thinking, believing I'll never finish this book. To counter that, I keep a Post-it note with a message from a fellow writer. It's a friendly reminder that if I stay consistent, even if I don't reach my goal for the day, I'll still be further along than when I started.

Photo courtesy of the author.

The original message included that I will have made magnificent progress. But when I'm caught up in the extreme belief that I'll never finish the book, that feels too big a shift for me to accept. So, I wrote the first part of the message (that I will make progress) on one Post-it note, and when I'm in a better feeling place, I read and accept the Post-it underneath, which reminds me that I've made magnificent progress.

Photo courtesy of the author.

Middle Think Is Reconnecting

Extremes are loud, and it's easy to get lost in the noise. Many of us haven't had the chance to find ourselves to begin with. Without a clear sense of who we are, we lack direction and get disconnected. Distracted by advertisements and other people's extreme views, we follow their lead while abandoning our own path.

When we focus on external influences instead of connecting with ourselves, we become fixated on extremes, believing they're the only way to live. This narrows our view, blinding us to possibilities that will align with our true values and desires. It creates inner turmoil and deep unhappiness, making it easy to dwell on the negative.

To stop the cycle, we need to reconnect with ourselves by clarifying our values and building awareness around the various roles we take on in life.

Value Setting

Values represent what's important to you. They shape your identity and give you a sense of purpose and direction. They also influence your attitudes, actions, and how you interact with others. For example, someone who values honesty will strive to tell the truth, even when it's uncomfortable or may lead to negative consequences.

A simple focus on values will help you reject the extremes in your environment and thoughts. But you aren't really "rejecting" the extremes; you're focusing your attention on what you want instead of what you don't want, leading to a more fulfilling and balanced life. Balance itself is a value and you're showing that you value balance by learning to middle think. Here are 11 other common values that will help you stay centered:

Moderation	Presence	Open-mindedness	Empathy
Integrity	Resilience	Self-reflection	Flexibility
Gratitude	Compassion	Curiosity	

When you value compassion and empathy, you focus on showing kindness and understanding toward yourself and others. This helps you appreciate different viewpoints and stops you from making extreme judgments. Curiosity and open-mindedness encourage you to seek out and consider various perspectives and nuanced views.

Valuing flexibility and resilience will help you adapt to new ideas and approaches. While setbacks may be frustrating, you prevent yourself from creating extreme narratives. Practicing gratitude will reduce the urge to compare yourself to idealistic lifestyles and extremes.

By reading this book and working to improve yourself, you show that you value moderation and presence. You also demonstrate integrity and self-reflection by taking the time to focus on your thoughts and feelings, ensuring they align with what truly matters to you.

Take some time now to consider what values are most important to you. How can you continue to integrate them into your life? For instance, if you value open-mindedness, how can you be more open to differing opinions?

_____

_____

_____

It's easy to lose sight of our values in the noise of extremes. So, if you see an advertisement suggesting you need to buy a lot of products to keep up with a trend, ask yourself, *Is this moderation?* Or if you stress about looking perfect on a date or with friends, ask, *Am I being present?* When you focus on what truly matters, you stay centered and grounded. The more you reconnect with yourself, the less anxious you will feel, encouraging you to continue to find balance.

Identity and Roles

Throughout our lives, we take on various identities. These roles can be self-defined or given to us by others. It starts before you're born, beginning with labels like your gender and race. You might be a "rainbow baby," "middle child," or a "happy accident." After birth, traits such as eye color, height, and weight add to your identity, along with the timing of your arrival—whether "premature," "right on time," or "post-term." To your parents, you're their child; to your grandparents, their grandchild.

As we grow, we embrace additional aspects of ourselves, like identifying with our hobbies or fandoms (e.g., gardener, Trekkie), and we adopt roles we may not realize, like those tied to mental health, like being an advocate or survivor.

Here are some common types of identities:

1. **Family:** mother, son, cousin, sibling
2. **Gender:** male, female, non-binary, transgender
3. **Sexual:** heterosexual, homosexual, bisexual, asexual
4. **Professional:** engineer, teacher, artist, technician
5. **Religious:** Christian, Muslim, Jewish, atheist
6. **National:** American, Brazilian, Australian
7. **Political:** Liberal, Conservative, Independent
8. **Physical:** tall, short, fit, plus-size, disabled
9. **Relationship:** single, married, co-parent
10. **Digital:** gamer, influencer, LinkedIn professional
11. **Educational:** college graduate, PhD candidate, lifelong learner

Sensationalized news often amplifies identities to create division, pitting men against women, Black against White, or immigrant against native. It even leverages generational identities, like Baby Boomers or Gen Z, to deepen generational divides.[31] Marketers also exploit relationship identities to sell products on Valentine's Day and family identities to craft campaigns, hoping to evoke a sense of emotional connection that drives you to buy their products.[32]

To stay connected with ourselves and to avoid falling victim to extremes and distracting marketing tactics, it's important to understand the many roles we have. Take a moment to reflect on your various identities. Remember, you might be a boss at work, but an employee to your supervisor. To your parents, you're still their child, and to your child, you're the parent.

Sometimes we take on so many identities that it's hard to keep up. We may become attached to a single identity, mistaking one aspect of who we are for our entire purpose—like a workaholic who struggles to relax or explore other interests.

While a new mother focuses on caring for her baby, neglecting all other aspects of herself can lead to burnout. People who lean too deeply into their religious identity may become intolerant of other viewpoints and rationalize their behavior, even when their faith advocates for love. And someone who overly identifies with their academic success may experience stunted personal growth and isolate themselves from those outside their field.

Similarly, while the "fat acceptance" movement had good intentions, it led some people to over-identify with their bodies, resulting in lower self-esteem disguised as "confidence." And a hyperfocus on your relationship status will lead to accepting poor treatment or feeling like a "nobody" without a partner. Even political identities are becoming extreme, with some people wrapping their cars, covering their homes, and dedicating their wardrobes to symbols of their favorite politician. And we've all seen hyper-dedicated sports fans go to extremes when their team loses, or music fandoms react intensely when their artist gets bad press.

When identity is taken to extremes, it creates an imbalance. This excessive focus leads to a limited sense of self and inner emptiness. To fill the gap, people may mimic exaggerated portrayals of their chosen identity seen in media, which only creates more inner conflict and blocks personal growth.

To avoid extremes, it's important to embrace the many sides of who you are. A holistic and well-rounded self-view allows us to appreciate all aspects of our identity, which helps us better understand others and build a deeper sense of self-love.

By building this compassion and balance within ourselves, we're more equipped to resist the extreme influences in our environment that distract us. Embracing who we are holistically also reduces the stress and anxiety that comes from trying to fit into roles that don't align with our values. We won't allow other people to define us with their extreme terms because we will be connected and in control of our own identities.

Connected

We all like to believe we're making choices that reflect who we really are, but it's tough to avoid the influence of our surroundings. Reconnecting with our true selves creates a protective barrier against these distractions, making us less vulnerable to being swayed by advertisements, sensationalized news, or social pressures dictating who we should be. While we may still get caught up in extremes, it's easier to return to center when we prioritize our values and know how we want to show up in our lives.

Middle Think Is Owning It

Who hasn't been teased for something they liked? Told their dreams were unrealistic? Or felt like they couldn't be vulnerable because others would perceive it as a sign of weakness? We're pressured to fit in, requiring us to abandon what we truly like and choose between "either-or" categories. This binary mindset doesn't just force us to ignore complexities; it also teaches us to reject anything labeled "bad," like sensitivity or unconventional preferences.

Instead of asking ourselves what brings us genuine joy, we chase symbols of success—the big house, the trendy lifestyle—thinking that's what will make us happy. Yet, the extravagant house may not be as important as we think; what we might truly seek is a space where we can relax with our loved ones. And we worry we won't be accepted if we don't follow trends, but to be happy, we need to focus on what genuinely resonates with us—not on what an editor at a fashion magazine tells us we should like.

To escape these limiting extremes, it's essential to reconnect with ourselves and trust that authentic connections will naturally follow. This requires us to embrace and "own" our true desires.

Likes and Dislikes

It's not easy to separate genuine interests from external pressures and influences, especially since many of us haven't had the freedom to explore our preferences. Instead, society has conditioned us to chase the idealized lifestyles we see on TV, social media, and advertisements, without taking the time to consider if they're what we truly want—or if we would want them if we hadn't been influenced.

With so many distractions, you might not know what you genuinely enjoy or realize that you've lost sight of your true preferences. A great starting point is to categorize the things in your life into what you like, dislike, and feel indifferent about. Consider everyday activities—like cooking, running errands, or exercising—and small things that bring you joy, such as lighting a candle, cuddling, or a favorite snack. Try not to think too deeply about it; just let the thoughts flow. Sometimes, it's the small things—like a morning routine or a favorite book—that hold the most meaning.

Sort your responses in the columns below.

Like	Indifferent	Dislike

Now do a high-level overview of your list. Do you notice any patterns? Are there things you're surprised you don't actually like? Anything in the "like" column surprise you?

_____

_____

_____

Acknowledging what you don't enjoy helps you focus on what truly brings joy. Is there anything on your "dislike" list that you can deprioritize in your life? Can you prioritize items on your "like" list? Are the things you feel indifferent about balanced?

_____

_____

_____

Unfortunately, we have to do things like laundry and dishes, even when we don't enjoy them. What things on your list do you need to accept as necessary parts of life, even if you don't like them? How can you make these tasks more enjoyable while doing them?

_____

_____

_____

Years ago, "watching movies and cuddling" were on my "like" list, while "potholes and traffic" went straight to my "dislike" list. And I realized how much I truly hated my daily commute so I looked for a job closer to home. For five years, I walked to work, and I used the extra time to create a cozy, relaxing home environment. Life became much happier with a few changes.

Luckily, I could make those adjustments. However, some of us have responsibilities that may prevent us from fully prioritizing what we enjoy. In those cases, it's important to accept the situation without getting stuck in negativity. Instead, look for small joys within your responsibilities and work them into your routine.

Ditching the "Or"

In the last section, we talked about balancing the multiple roles we take on. It's equally important to own your multiple interests and identities, even when they conflict with common expectations. This means letting go of the idea that we need to fit into a single category and embracing the reality that both we and those around us can exist in the "and."

You can be into heavy metal and cuddling. Muscular and sensitive. Practical and willing to take healthy risks. You can be anti-abortion and still support a woman's right to choose. A feminist without hating men. Christian and supportive of LGBTQ rights. A fan of a Taylor Swift song without being a Swiftie. You can enjoy sex without being promiscuous. Be strong and still cry. Open to help and not be weak. You can be an introvert and a leader. Feminine and love weightlifting. Smart and still make dumb decisions. Single and genuinely happy. Young and wise. You can feel happy and sad at the same time. Nervous and excited. A nice person and still say "no." A good employee and still leave for a better job.

One of my favorite media portrayals of this is from the show *Beverly Hills, 90210.*[33] Donna advocates for safe sex and supports making condoms freely available at school. She stands by this position even when others judge her and assume she's sexually active. Seeing her enthusiasm, her boyfriend David misinterprets her stance and assumes she's ready to take their relationship to the next level.

Later, when they're hanging out alone, David, like any typical 17-year-old virgin, eagerly expects things to move forward, but Donna just wants to order pizza and relax. Confused and disappointed, David questions why she would support access to condoms if she isn't planning to use them. Donna explains that even though she supports others' right to control their own choices, it doesn't mean she's ready—she's waiting for marriage.

This story is a great reminder that just because someone supports an issue doesn't mean they're making the same choices for themselves. David's assumptions were based on his own misunderstandings, but Donna didn't need to change her views or preferences to match his expectations.

Of course, there are *some* exceptions. If someone is sending mixed signals and constantly changing their mind, then that means they're truly confused. But if someone is clear about their boundaries and consistent in expressing their preferences, the confusion is often because of the other person's expectations, not mixed messages.

Embracing our "ands" helps us own our likes and release the extreme idea that we need to choose between genuine parts of who we are. What may seem like conflicting qualities are not actually at odds; they only appear that way because of the rigid standards set by our environment. This mindset not only supports your growth; when we stop making assumptions and ask others about their preferences, we open the door for true understanding and authentic connections.

Embracing Complexities

Owning who we are means embracing our complexities and rejecting the pressure to fit into narrow categories. It requires us to separate what we truly enjoy from what we've been taught to want and honor our genuine preferences even if they don't align with the "ideal" lifestyles we see around us. The path to self-acceptance isn't straightforward. You may feel silly when you try new things, and you may discover the things you thought would make you happy really don't. The goal is to reconnect and find what truly brings you joy, even in small ways.

Once we understand our own needs and interests, we show up more fully and confidently in our relationships and communities. We'll stop feeling torn between extremes and embrace the nuances that make us who we are. This not only strengthens our relationship with ourselves, but also inspires others to embrace their own unique identities. And while it can feel vulnerable to be true to ourselves, it leads to a more balanced and fulfilling life—one where we define what happiness looks like for us.

Middle Think Is Redefining

Extremes influence how we define words. Food and emotions are over-simplified and quickly labeled as "good" or "bad," leaving no room for nuance. Concepts like "balance" and "positivity" are reduced to singular, unattainable ideals, ignoring the fact that most ideas are fluid and situational.

Since we use language to shape our worldview, extreme definitions limit our understanding and ability to accurately express our experiences. They lead to rigid thinking, preventing us from seeing complexities and pushing us to interpret reality in black-and-white terms.

To create a balanced mindset, we need to define words more accurately to reflect our authentic experiences, recognizing that, like most concepts, their meanings often exist in shades of gray.

Shades of Meaning

Concepts are rarely black or white. Most ideas, like food or the habits we form, exist in a spectrum of complexity and nuance. What may be beneficial in one context can be harmful in another, requiring us to approach decisions with flexibility and balance. For instance, working out is beneficial for mental and physical health, but when taken to an extreme it can be detrimental and a way to escape or avoid facing challenges. And certain foods don't provide nutritional value, but they can be a nice way to treat ourselves in moderation. Understanding this nuance allows us to move away from extremes and embrace a more open-minded perspective.

To see beyond rigid definitions, we need to recognize the shades of meaning. Think of it like you're choosing a color to paint a room. You wouldn't think of the colors as "good" or "bad." It's about what best suits the room's lighting, size, and purpose.

We often see concepts in extreme shades, like in movies with jealous lovers acting irrationally. In real life, if a partner is acting violently because of envy, then it's a sign of an unhealthy relationship and time to move on. But if you feel envious when your partner isn't doing anything to cause envy, it can be a sign that you love your partner and need to work on managing your feelings. The more you accept envy as a representation of your own insecurities the easier it will be to manage.

Envy, when channeled positively, motivates us to grow, set goals, and work toward what we truly want. Say you feel envious of an influencer with an athletic build. It may signal a need to work out and improve your own health. If you work on your fitness routine and realize you're not willing to go to the extreme lengths the influencer took to achieve their body, you may find that your envy isn't as strong as you thought. This realization can help you appreciate your current body more, as you learn to prioritize your own well-being over unrealistic standards.

Here are three shades of concepts that are commonly defined in extremes:

Positivity:

Toxic: Forces fake cheerfulness and invalidates emotions.	*Optimistic:* Balances hope with a realistic view of challenges.	*Authentic:* Embraces all emotions, allowing for genuine resilience.

Gratitude:

Toxic: Demands gratitude in all situations, even in pain or hardship.	*Obligatory:* Expresses thanks out of habit, not genuine feeling.	*Authentic:* Truly appreciates both big and small positives.

Lazy: --

| *Toxic:* Avoids all responsibility, leading to missed opportunities. | *Procrastination:* Takes breaks but feels guilty, preventing true relaxation. | *Restful:* Takes intentional breaks to recharge, balancing rest with productivity. |

For simplicity, I listed three shades here, but there can be several shades of a word depending on the situation. And the word "toxic" was used to describe the more negative side of concepts because it was concise, but "toxic" can be replaced with "counterproductive" because when we define concepts in extremes, we're usually hindering ourselves from achieving our goals.

Other common concepts, like weakness, anxiety, and perfection, follow a similar spectrum. Weakness can be toxic when it leads to avoidance, but it can also reflect temporary struggles or a valuable opportunity to grow. Anxiety can be debilitating, but it can also be constructive when it drives preparation and focus. Perfection becomes toxic when it's obsessive, but it can be balanced by striving for improvement while accepting flaws.

So the next time you're being "lazy," ask yourself if you're avoiding responsibilities or taking a much needed break. And if your anxiety feels debilitating, look into ways to increase your confidence and reduce the intensity.

"Good" or "Bad"

The idea of labeling concepts as "good" or "bad" is extreme, but it also highlights something very important: the way we view things is the way they are. This means something isn't "good" or "bad" until we put that label on it.

We typically consider anger a "bad" emotion because we witness angry people on TV yelling and acting violently. But it isn't the emotion, it's what you do with it that counts. And just because someone on a TV show—or in real life—lacks the ability to manage their anger doesn't mean anger is "bad." It also doesn't mean that person is "bad." It just shows they lack emotional management.

When you channel emotions like anger positively, they become a valuable resource for growth, providing insights into your mindset and helping you reject extremes. If you're angry at an inanimate object for not working properly, is it because someone oversold it? If you're angry at a situation, is it because you feel you can't get out of it? Working through the emotions and where they come from will help you reduce their intensity.

Reducing the "good" and "bad" labels will help you find a more balanced perspective. Sure, things like rejection can hurt, but it isn't inherently "bad," because it's also a sign that you tried. And yes, some foods are better for you than others, but sometimes we need to just order the darn chocolate cake and take a moment to enjoy the pleasure of it.

Empowerment in Perspective

Reducing the intensity we attach to certain words also decreases the pressure we place on ourselves when others use these labels to define us. It helps us manage our thoughts and responses, giving us control over the narrative, and prevents others from manipulating or provoking us. For example, when someone calls you "selfish" for not helping them move or tries to provoke you by calling you "weak," recognizing these terms as part of a spectrum helps you remain grounded and true to yourself.

Similarly, understanding that concepts show up differently across different aspects of life allows us to accept ourselves and others more fully. While you might struggle with vulnerability in romantic relationships, it doesn't negate the vulnerability you display in other areas. Life is dynamic, and our experiences and behaviors will naturally ebb and flow. This doesn't mean that we're inconsistent or flawed; it means we're adapting and growing, like we're meant to.

While we've only covered a few concepts here, it's important to continually question how you define things in your life and if you might be viewing them in an extreme way. Make a conscious effort to define concepts in shades of meaning rather than labeling them as simply "good" or "bad." Before jumping to conclusions, take a moment to recognize the nuances in your thoughts and experiences. By doing

so, you empower yourself to embrace complexity, build self-acceptance, and create deeper connections with others.

Middle Think Is Turning Down the Pressure

Straight "A's," constant career growth, curated social media feeds, the need to always look our best. In a world dominated by extremes there is a lot of pressure. We're expected to conform, learn new skills at lightning speed, excel in everything, and find the perfect partner and home—all while sporting an ideal morning outfit during our flawless workout and morning routine.

This makes us feel like we're walking on eggshells, one tiny mistake away from ruining *everything*. It results in stress, burnout, and worry—fear of looking unprepared, failing, not measuring up, and being ourselves.

Balanced thinking involves releasing the idea that you need to be perfect. You accept that humans are fundamentally flawed, and learning new skills takes time—sometimes several years. While society has conditioned you to see this as negative, in The Middle, you understand that learning is rewarding, regardless of the time it takes. So let's talk about turning down the pressure to create space for improvement and growth.

Perfection Doesn't Exist

From an early age, we're conditioned to chase perfection and led to believe that anything less than ideal means we're failing. This mindset is not only unrealistic, it's also detrimental to our growth. Easing the rigid expectations starts with accepting that perfection doesn't exist. While this may seem obvious, you might aim for perfection without realizing it. It can show up as procrastination where you put off tasks because you worry the result won't be good enough. You might fixate on minor details or feel like you can't trust others to do things right, leading you to take on everything yourself. Perfectionism can also cause you to constantly criticize your work, avoid experiences that are new, or seek reassurance even when you don't need it. You may apologize for minor mistakes or feel guilty for taking time to relax.

It's tough to break perfectionistic tendencies because society has normalized them. Here are three things to keep in mind while you reduce the pressure:

Permission Not to Be Perfect

A lot of us need permission we didn't know we needed.

You have permission not to be perfect. You don't need to know everything or excel in every aspect of life. It's okay not to have the perfect morning routine, relationship, or career. It's okay if you don't want to travel to remote locations in Tanzania or if you have interests that don't align with society's ideals. It's okay if you're voting for a politician but can't refute every argument against their policies. It's okay if you like a TV show or a sports team and you don't know the stats for their 1973 season or the middle name of their most popular player in 1952.

You have permission to make mistakes and not know something—unless, of course, it's literally your job to know it. The key isn't in what you know, but in recognizing what you don't know and working to learn. It's not about being perfect; it's about taking responsibility for your mistakes and striving to do better. We often hear these truths, but they can fade into the background. We need to remind ourselves daily that we don't have to be perfect and encourage others to do the same, as even those who advocate for progress over perfection can unknowingly seek perfection themselves.

Giving yourself permission also means gently reminding others that you aren't perfect. People sometimes forget that it's okay for us to change our minds and may be surprised if you shift your stance on an issue or topic. The meaning of life is to learn and grow.

Mistakes are Learning Opportunities

Viewing mistakes in extremes—where one missed opportunity or failed relationship feels like a total loss—creates pressure for perfection. To ease the intensity, we need to remind ourselves that mistakes are part of growth and that there will be opportunities all during our lives as long as we stay open to them. Instead of seeing failures as a reflection of your worth, view them as a chance to learn. This doesn't mean mistakes aren't frustrating; it means working through that frustration and striving to avoid repeating those errors.

When I wrote my first book, I made a lot of mistakes and spent money I wish I hadn't. In writing this book, I rushed the process and ended up rewriting it. You're reading the second edition; the first one didn't even make it to publication. On any given day, I make multiple mistakes in writing. The key isn't the mistakes I make; it's how I manage them. I've learned where not to spend money in the writing process, and I believe this version of the book will shine and help you best.

Most people also make mistakes in relationships. In a culture that promotes the belief that we need someone else to feel whole, we often feel pressured to be in a relationship, mistaking attention for genuine connection. However, the biggest mistake you can make is not prioritizing yourself over a relationship. Instead, view a relationship as an opportunity for growth. If it doesn't work out, take a moment to reflect on what you will miss and what you won't. This balanced approach will not only help you seek a partner with the traits you desire but also empower you to leave behind what no longer serves you.

Forgiveness

Self-forgiveness is key to breaking the cycle of perfectionism. This looks like acknowledging past mistakes, seeing what you can learn from them, and then forgiving yourself for not doing your best. This doesn't mean excusing your behavior, but it means recognizing that you're human and that mistakes happen.

Part of self-forgiveness is letting go of the rigid and unrealistic standards you set for yourself and forgiving yourself for being unkind when you make mistakes. This looks like taking a deep breath when you do something dumb, accepting that you didn't know better, and committing to do better moving forward.

Unfortunately, growth often means repeating the same mistakes a few times before finally changing—you know, like messaging an ex even though you know it's a waste of time. But even though it may look like you're making the same mistake, you're likely doing it to a lesser extent. And the more you forgive yourself, the more you will reduce the emotional impact behind mistakes, and the more you will effectively correct them. Take a moment now to think of a time you were hard on yourself for a simple mistake and forgive yourself for that unkindness.

Not only does self-forgiveness help, but seeking forgiveness from others also allows us to regain balance and reconnect with ourselves. It's crucial not to force forgiveness and to accept that others may not forgive you, even for minor issues. If someone chooses not to forgive you, it doesn't mean you're a bad person; it may simply mean that the relationship is no longer a good fit. We must respect the other person's decision and understand that there will be better, more forgiving relationships ahead.

Flaws and All

In trying to be all things to all people, we lose ourselves. We spend our time keeping up appearances and pretending to be happy and perfect when we're not. And we allow others to define us in extremes and judge us for not knowing what we were never taught.

Remember, no one is born with all the answers. If you weren't taught something, then naturally, you wouldn't know it. This doesn't make you uneducated or dumb. However, it's in your best interest to learn what's relevant to your job and your life.

And if someone labels you harshly based on a single mistake, that says more about their unhealthy mindset than it does about you. But if you keep making the same mistake, it suggests that some changes may be necessary.

Turning down the pressure and focusing on self-compassion and forgiveness takes strength and courage. There's no one more powerful than a person who has their own back—even when they're frustrated with themselves for slipping up.

Middle Think Is Embracing Uncertainty

When will I feel more confident? What if things don't go according to plan? How will I know if I'm on the right track?... Uncertainty is scary. This fear can keep us stuck in extremes because even though they aren't healthy for us, the extremes shield us from the unknown.

The desire for perfection prevents us from trying new things. Being rigid and unforgiving keeps us from getting hurt. Letting a minor inconvenience ruin our day keeps us from embracing happiness and the scary potential of losing it. But our efforts to control uncertainty often lead to extreme thinking, limiting our thoughts. Life becomes rigid.

Middle thinking is embracing the uncertainty and allowing the nuance. It's accepting that we're doing the best we can; we may get hurt again, but in the end, we can and we will continue to move forward in our lives.

Uncertainty Is the Worst

Extremes make us forget that two things can be true at once. You can be excited and also sad, nervous and scared, while also being strong and resilient. Forgetting we can be two things at once pressures us to reject how uncomfortable uncertainty is, or that, for lack of a better phrase, it sucks.

Uncertainty is uncomfortable; it's scary. It isn't something anyone would choose. But you need to embrace uncertainty because it's a guarantee, and in life there are more things you can't control, more things that are uncertain, than are.

People who embrace uncertainty are powerful. During times of uncertainty, we discover who we are, increase resilience, and get things done. We build confidence, and yes, sometimes we cry on the couch for days and want to give up, but we get back out there. Here are some techniques to help you manage.

The One Word

This technique combines breathing exercises with vocalization. I came up with it while I was managing difficult emotions that came from uncertainty. Feeling uncomfortable, I hoped a therapy session would help, but I still felt anxious. My therapist suggested that I "sit with" my feelings, which can be incredibly difficult to do. The intense emotions made me want to scream. Instead, I sat on my couch, leaned my head back, and said, "This sucks." It felt good, so I said it again, using a vocal fry to emphasize the "u" and make the word come out longer. And I realized I needed to take deep breaths to sustain this, and that the breathing helped reduce the emotional intensity.

Choose one word or sound—like "sucks," "ugh," "f*ck," or any other—take a deep breath from your chest, and then let the word out, extending the vowel sound while releasing your breath. If the word takes a second to say, stretch it to 10-15 seconds. Take another deep breath and repeat this a few times until the heaviness lifts. By the time I'm finished, I end up laughing and feeling better. While the uncertainty might still annoy me, the lightness helps me move past it without saying or doing anything I might regret.

The Continual Reminder

Uncertainty is scary, especially if we're vulnerable, putting ourselves out there, or working toward something we deeply want. Having a mantra is incredibly beneficial as it acts as a friendly reminder that this uncertainty, and the discomfort it brings, is only temporary.

Mantras are phrases that help us focus and create positive change. You can have one or more mantras, as different sayings may serve you at different times and in various areas of your life. Two that were effective for me are "I am doing the best I can" and "I am safe." Just these two quick reminders helped me feel grounded when I was uncertain or nervous about trying something new.

Here are some other mantras you can use when facing uncertainty:

- I can handle whatever comes my way.
- I trust myself to figure things out.
- It's okay not to have all the answers.
- I am learning and growing every day.
- I am strong enough to face uncertainty.
- I choose to focus on what I can control and let go of what I can't.
- I believe in my ability to adapt and overcome challenges.
- Uncertainty is a normal part of life, and I can navigate it.
- I embrace uncertainty as an opportunity for growth and discovery.
- This too shall pass.

Using your mantra will help you come back to center, allowing you to face uncertainty with greater balance. You can use any of the mantras mentioned above or choose your own; the important thing is to have one. Remember to use your mantra even in low-stakes situations that make you anxious, like making appointments, as well as in more significant moments, like preparing for a public speech.

The Regulars

Avoiding uncertainty leads to negative coping mechanisms to handle our discomfort, like binge drinking, binge watching, mindlessly scrolling through social media, or impulse buying. And while these things can temporarily distract us, they leave us feeling worse in the long run (e.g., hangovers and clutter), and can lead us to more black-and-white and extreme thinking.

To stay balanced, we need to swap out the unhealthy coping with healthy coping mechanisms. Here are a few ideas:

1. Moving Your Body. Take a walk and concentrate on being present. Notice the scenery around you and enjoy moving your body. This will clear your mind and reduce stress.[34]
2. Making a Control List. Make a list of things you can control, can somewhat control, and cannot control. This grounds you and helps you get a better handle on the uncertainties of life.
3. Visualizing Positive Outcomes. In uncertain situations, imagine positive outcomes. Focus on managing your thoughts and lean into optimism instead of pessimism.
4. Practicing the ICE Method. Use the ICE (Identify, Challenge, Embrace) Method on difficult thoughts to build self-awareness and help you return to a calm and centered state.
5. Connecting with Others. Call a friend or family member and ask how they're doing. Building connections can help you feel supported and less isolated.
6. Imagining Your Thoughts as Clouds. Visualize your thoughts floating away like clouds in the sky. This can help you release any lingering negativity.
7. Massages or Breathing Exercises. Engage in activities that bring you into your body and help you feel centered. This can include getting a massage or practicing deep breathing exercises.

Healthy coping mechanisms help you build skills you can use throughout your life. When you get out of your mind and into action, you look for ways to achieve your goals. You will connect with others and find different perspectives. This positive looping will help you manage uncertainty more effectively and will lead to a healthier, more fulfilling life. By replacing negative habits with positive ones, you can build resilience and maintain a balanced outlook even in the face of challenges.

Embracing and Expecting Uncertainty

Managing uncertainty prevents you from falling into extremes, like believing that *everyone* is untrustworthy, that the world is doomed, or that you'll never feel better. It helps you regulate your emotions and return to a centered state. Instead of sending long texts or saying things you might regret, you can sit with the uncomfortable feelings, let them pass, and find that those emotions become less intense over time. By doing this, you're building resilience and emotional regulation—two skills that have been life-changing for me and will be for you too.

Most people prefer to have control and avoid uncertainty. But uncertainty is unavoidable. You don't have to love it, but for your health you need to at least embrace it. If not, it's going to consume you, or you'll exhaust yourself trying to control things you can't. While facing uncertainty may be painful at the moment, it's the most pragmatic option. The other choices will ultimately lead to greater hurt in the long run.

Middle Think Is Abundance

We've all been told what we "should" want. That we need a relationship to feel complete, or that being the center of attention is necessary for fulfillment. But who decides these things? Why can't we define success for ourselves?

Extreme thinking limits our perceptions and what we believe we can achieve. Instead of recognizing our unique strengths, we adopt a scarcity mindset, thinking we're forced to choose between limited options. It's no wonder people believe that they can't pursue their goals, or that they'll *never* find anyone better than their ex.

When we accept these limiting thoughts as truths, we miss out on new opportunities, reinforcing the belief that temporary setbacks are permanent. To think with balance—and reject extremes—we need to focus on ditching the beliefs that limit us and focus on empowerment and abundance.

Limited Thinking

Limiting beliefs aren't always extreme. Sometimes they show up as quiet doubts or invisible barriers—like assuming we aren't smart enough to pursue a passion. They focus on what we lack, emphasizing flaws and limitations, creating a loop of self-criticism that makes our worldview small and keeps us from taking action.

For example, a large majority of people believe that depression results from a chemical imbalance in the brain,[35] even though scientists have never proven it.[36] People who hold this belief may feel powerless, thinking medication is their only solution. While medication can be helpful, actual change often involves more holistic approaches like managing thoughts, staying active, and building healthy routines.

The same goes for outdated ideas about gender roles—believing one gender is more emotional or intelligent than the other only narrows our potential and keeps us divided. There's no evidence to support that one gender is more intelligent or emotional than the other,[37] yet these beliefs are common. Women give up on their passions in STEM because they don't believe they're smart enough, while men often avoid showing emotions because it means they are, gasp, acting like a woman.

The problem is, when we're stuck in these limiting beliefs, we don't see the abundance of other possibilities. These beliefs are toxic and focus on what you can't do, emphasizing flaws and undermining confidence. They create a sense of helplessness, leading to inaction and paralysis.

Empowering Beliefs

To work through these limitations, we need to shift our perspective to beliefs that empower us. Here is a comparison between the two:

Limiting Belief	Empowering Belief
Scarcity: Resources and opportunities are scarce, requiring competition.	Abundance: There are ample resources and opportunities for everyone.
Negative: Focuses on pessimism, problems, and potential drawbacks.	Positive: Focuses on optimism, solutions, and benefits.
Closed: Resistant to new ideas or perspectives.	Open: Willing to consider new ideas and experiences.

Self-Critical: Harsh self-judgment, focusing on flaws.	Self-Compassionate: Kindness toward yourself, especially during challenges.
Confidence-Diminishing: Undermines self-esteem and fuels self-doubt.	Confidence-Building: Encourages belief in your abilities.
Paralyzing: Leads to inaction and a lack of progress.	Actionable: Motivates proactive steps toward achieving goals.

Empowering beliefs focus on growth, learning, and resilience. Not to be confused with magical thinking or unrealistic beliefs, empowering beliefs motivate you to take proactive steps toward your goals. Instead of thinking something is too difficult to achieve, you would ask yourself what roadblocks are in your way and how you can overcome them. If you feel inadequate or that you aren't deserving of love, remind yourself that everyone deserves to succeed, and you have the potential to achieve great things.

Asking Why

Limiting beliefs are deeply ingrained and accepted as truth; we might not recognize them or that there are alternative ways to think. It's essential to learn how to identify these beliefs, and the best way to do that is with curiosity and asking a simple question: Why?

If you think you can't accomplish a goal, ask yourself why? Did you try before and fail? Why? Did you have unrealistic expectations of the time it would take to complete the goal because of disingenuous marketing (e.g., Get your dream body in 10 days)? Do you need to change your lifestyle and be more active?

Maybe it's a goal that seems far-fetched. Why? We want to stay within reason here, so a goal wouldn't be to be the "Queen/King of the Universe" with everyone admiring you, but you can want a goal of a loving and monogamous relationship. This may seem unrealistic to those who cheat or believe loyalty in relationships is rare but healthy, loyal relationships do exist.

Asking "Why?" also helps when others try to limit you. If someone tells you that you can't achieve something, ask why. Is it because they couldn't, and now they're projecting their limitations onto you? Or do they hold rigid beliefs about gender roles or success? Why? Do they have a rigid mentality behind gender or other roles so they don't like you thinking differently? Why? (Hot Tip: It's about control.)

Asking "why" opens the door to understanding the real barriers in your way. For example, if a woman aims for a leadership role, she may face obstacles. Why? Because people have traditionally assigned leadership roles to men. Does that mean she can't break through? No. Why? Because barriers are being challenged, and progress is being made.

Awareness and Abundance in Time

A limiting belief that holds people back when focusing on their thoughts is the idea that they are their thoughts. But you aren't your thoughts; you are the awareness of them. By making that separation, you can prevent yourself from becoming overwhelmed. If you hold an extreme belief, remind yourself that the awareness of that belief is an opportunity to change it.

Sure, that job you interviewed for might have been great, but it doesn't mean you won't have opportunities for better jobs in the future. And yes, that relationship could have been wonderful, but there's a reason you broke up, and you can find love again when you're open to it.

Learning about how you may have been limiting yourself can be helpful, but it can also be challenging. You may realize areas where you've been holding yourself back or have trouble discovering that a current belief is limiting because it feels so normal. The goal isn't to recognize and change every limiting belief, but to focus on abundance, especially when someone tries to force a scarcity narrative.

Middle Think Is
a Love Letter

Ten years ago, I didn't know what all-or-nothing thinking was. I didn't focus on my thoughts or realize the importance of them. And I had no idea how much the constant extremes were impacting my life. It didn't occur to me to seek out anything different or make any changes because it was my normal. I just assumed life was rigid and that things were doomed and I would *never* find the relationships, love, or happiness that I longed for.

Like many others, I grew up in an environment where one mistake would be held over my head and my accomplishments would be ignored. I was encouraged to be perfect and punished when I wasn't. It was scary and it was painful because the entire time I was being taken away from myself.

As I grew, I carried these extremes with me. A heavy weight on my life, I would cut off relationships at even the slightest disagreement because I figured there was no point; it was over. I would beat myself up for saying even one wrong word because I figured others would judge me. And I would see nightmare horror stories on the news and social media, thinking they were a reflection of the entire world.

I believed I wasn't beautiful enough, not smart enough, never enough. Ignoring my true preferences because I was scared I would be considered "too much." I would give until I had nothing left. I was exhausted, depressed, heartbroken, and even in the largest crowds, felt utterly alone.

Until one day enough was enough. I was tired of bullying myself with the words I heard as a kid. Tired of thinking *never*. Exhausted from feeling like I was the only one in the world who valued loyalty and kindness.

So I stopped and asked myself, "Why?" Why can't I have the relationship, life, and happiness I want? Why can't I pursue my dreams and accomplish goals? And that's the day I discovered The Middle. The day I realized I can have a life I love. That the world is better than others, social media, and the news make it out to be. That most people don't act with malice.

From that day on, I prioritized looking for all-or-nothing thinking identifiers in my vocabulary and softening my everyday internal language. When I went through a breakup, instead of thinking the person was selfish or wrong, I would think they were acting selfishly and even though the relationship was no longer a good fit, we were once together for a reason. I would then focus on what I wanted in the next relationship—and what I didn't.

And I realized the only extremes in this world are the extreme mindsets. The ones that make us lose relevance of time because they tell us that one mistake will end it all, or one moment is the most important. I also learned that while those mindsets are loud, they're fragile and weak and the only power they have is the power I give them.

While I wish I could say I no longer get caught up in extremes, it still happens now and then. There are times I've cried out in frustration. I've sent long texts impulsively when my emotions got the best of me, regretting it later. And there have been times I wanted to give up. Times when I was going to give up. But then after some rest, I continued my quest to find The Middle again.

Because there are also times I cried out of joy. Jumped up and down in my kitchen in excitement because I changed my response and didn't beat myself up for a simple mistake. Times I apologized to someone for my extreme reaction, and even though they wouldn't forgive me, I was still proud of how far I'd come. Days where I would walk around the city and enjoy being. Moments where the intensity calmed and I realized life wasn't so bad.

Then there were the days of grief that came with realizing the missed opportunities and life I could have had if not for thinking in these extremes. Going through the bittersweet process of saying goodbye to the former version of myself that I needed to leave behind to get to where I needed to go next. I loved her; she protected me.

At times, I still feel like I will never be good enough. And even though I'm putting myself out there and sharing my writing with the world, which takes a lot of vulnerability, I was recently told I'm not vulnerable "enough." But I won't allow someone's misguided assessment stop me.

I learned it's okay to lean into softness. And it's okay to be scared and "not enough" for others. All that matters is that I'm enough for myself. Because, quite frankly, I *am* terrified. Scared that my books won't be well received, nervous that the infomercial in the beginning will be too confusing, wondering if I will need to give up writing and go back to a career. Unsure about the world. Wondering if I will find a healthy relationship. When in that relationship my anxiety will mess things up, or if my partner will be unfaithful or have a second family like the plot to that one movie.

People may try to convince you that fear is weakness, but I know from experience that acknowledging fear is strength. The nervousness isn't what matters; it's what you do with it that counts. I just finished my second book! By sharing parts of my story and showing you a new way of thinking, I hope to help you face some of your fears too.

Let this book remind you that someone is rooting for your success. I hope you will make the ugly art or embrace looking silly in a dance class and experience the joy and laughter that extremes have stolen from us. That you'll embrace your complexities and ask for forgiveness even when it's tough.

The process of finding The Middle, while painful, is incredibly rewarding. You will learn that you're in the middle of your life. You are becoming. And you may be confused, want to give up; you may give up. But the only thing that matters is that you get back up again.

With love,
Lyndsey

Bonus: Middle Think Is Knowing Dark Psychology

"Dark psychology" is a dramatic way of describing tactics that are used to manipulate, control, or exploit others. People like Robert Greene encourage these methods with books like *The 48 Laws of Power*, where manipulation is framed as a path to personal gain. People use them in interpersonal relationships, negotiations, and marketing.

One key aspect of dark psychology is all-or-nothing thinking, where people simplify situations by dismissing emotions and reactions. This approach ignores the complexity of feelings and forces people into extreme positions, making it seem like there are only two choices. It can lead to invalidation, making us question our own reality, wondering if we're overreacting or misinterpreting things.

This type of manipulation can lower self-esteem, distort your sense of reality, and even trap you in unhealthy relationships or poor decisions—like signing up for those long-term memberships or extended warranties we all regret.

Recognizing and challenging manipulative tactics is essential for protecting yourself from being controlled or coerced. When you identify these tactics, you avoid being trapped by limited options and maintain control over your decisions. It will also give you the opportunity to assess whether certain people or relationships are healthy for you.

I split the tactics into three categories—emotional manipulation, pressure, and distortion. Below, you'll find explanations, examples, and a middle thinking response for each to help you understand and address them.

Emotional Manipulation

… involves exploiting someone's emotions to make them feel guilty, inadequate, or pressured. Manipulators often frame situations in extremes, forcing you to choose between two rigid options. A balanced response can help you assert your needs and boundaries.

Guilt Tripping: "If you loved me, you'd do this for me."
Middle Think Response: "I understand you're upset, but my feelings matter too. I want to help, but I can't meet your expectations."

Emotional Blackmail: "If you don't do this, I'll be devastated and won't forgive you."
Middle Think Response: "I hear how strongly you feel, but threatening me isn't helpful. Let's find a solution that works for both of us."

Gaslighting: "You're overreacting; it's not a big deal."
Middle Think Response: "You may not think it's a big deal, but it's important to me. Let's acknowledge that my feelings matter."

A common limiting belief is that you're responsible for other people's emotions or that you "made" them "feel that way." And it's understandable that if you do something hurtful you will cause someone pain, but you aren't responsible for anyone else's feelings. When faced with emotional manipulation, reverse the situation. Consider if you'd say the words spoken to you.

Pressure Tactics

… use threats, demands, or ultimatums to force compliance. They create a false sense of urgency, leaving you feeling like there are limited options. Responding to these tactics requires either/or thinking and asserting a balanced perspective.

Coercion: "If you don't agree with me, you're against me."

Middle Think Response: "We can disagree without being on opposing sides. Let's find common ground."

Ultimatums: "Do what I want, or I'll cut you off."
Middle Think Response: "It's hurtful to hear that. Let's talk about what's bothering you instead of making threats."

Withholding: "If you don't do as I say, I'll give you the silent treatment."
Middle Think Response: "Shutting down communication won't help. Let's work through this together."

Pressure tactics are common in politics and political discussion. Someone using this tactic might say, "Anyone who disagrees with me is dumb or weak." These tactics can also be non-verbal. Instead of communicating, someone might use the silent treatment to exert pressure without stating it. Remind yourself that what people say is what they think, and ask yourself if their opinion matters.

Distortion Tactics

… twist reality to make situations seem worse than they are, pressuring you to agree with an extreme view. They work by exaggerating or altering facts, making you see things through a skewed perspective. Responding effectively involves identifying and challenging these distortions and focusing on a more balanced, realistic view.

Overgeneralizing: "You always mess things up."
Middle Think Response: "I made a mistake this time, but saying I always mess up isn't fair. Let's focus on how I can improve."

Selective Perception: "You never contribute anything valuable."
Middle Think Response: "That's not true. I've contributed in the past, and I'm doing my best now. Let's talk about what's needed."

False Dilemma: "You either do it my way or fail."
Middle Think Response: "There are more than two options. Let's explore other possibilities that work for both of us."

Self-Aggrandizement: "You'll never find someone who loves you like I do."

Middle Think Response: "I value what we've shared, but it's not fair to say no one else could love me. Love should be about support, not control."

Manipulative Comparisons: "Everyone else can do this perfectly; why can't you?"
Middle Think Response: "I'm doing my best, and comparing me to others isn't helpful. Let's focus on what I can do and how I can improve."

Distortion tactics often appear in song lyrics and melodramatic movies, and someone might pick them up from their environment. While this doesn't make it okay, understanding their source can be helpful. You don't want to end an otherwise healthy relationship just because the media influenced someone.

The Call Is Coming From Inside the House

Unfortunately, we sometimes use these manipulative tactics on ourselves. For example, we might believe we'll *never* find anyone better than an ex, or fail to recognize our successes, thinking we're *always* falling short. Recognizing when we're being self-critical and applying middle thinking can help us regain balance:

Overgeneralizing: "I always mess things up."
Middle Think Response: "I've made mistakes, but that doesn't mean I always fail. I can learn from this."

False Dilemma: "If I don't do everything perfectly, I'm a failure."
Middle Think Response: "It's not all-or-nothing. I'm making progress, even if it's not perfect."

Self-Depreciation: "No one will ever love me like my ex did."
Middle Think Response: "That relationship was meaningful, but it doesn't mean I can't find love again. We had wonderful moments, but there were aspects I won't miss. I can experience love in new ways."

It's important to recognize when these tactics are affecting you, both from your environment and your own thoughts. This helps keep your mind a safe space for clear thinking and creativity. Sometimes, simply getting out of bed and making a little more progress than the day before—even if it's less than you hoped—is all you need. It's the mindset I used to finish this very book!

General Defense

Responding to manipulation can be draining, especially when a tactic works, and you later realize you didn't handle it the way you wanted. It can also be hard to recognize manipulation because these behaviors are so common in everyday life. Subtle pressures, like advertisements that target our insecurities, try to sway us daily. But not every frustrating interaction is manipulative—sometimes, people act out of exhaustion or poor communication. For example, if a partner says, "We never go out anymore," it could be them expressing a feeling rather than trying to control the situation. And some people mimic TV behaviors without realizing how toxic they can be. It's important to take context into consideration and to remember that most people don't act with malice.

The responses I shared above are just suggestions. No response, or simple words like "ah," "okay," or "sure" can be enough. If someone tries to provoke you by saying that not doing what they want makes you weak, responding with a calm "okay" can completely disarm them.

Once you recognize manipulation tactics, you'll gain the power to reject false narratives without letting them affect you. And you'll be surprised how people change when they realize they can't control your emotions or manipulate you.

Templates

ICE Method

Situation Nickname:_____

Identify

Describe the situation. Write as much detail as you can.

_____

_____

_____

_____

_____

_____

What are the extreme or all-or-nothing thoughts? Can you identify where they came from? Are you using any identifiers in your internal dialogue?

_____

_____

_____

Challenge

Are you making assumptions? Do you have any facts to back up your thoughts?

_____

_____

_____

What are some middle thinking thoughts you can have? What would you say to a friend if they were in the same situation?

_____

_____

_____

Evaluate

How will replacing the extreme thought with a more balanced one help you reach your goals?

_____

_____

_____

Are there any actions you can take to get out of the extremes? What's stopping you from changing?

_____

_____

_____

ICE Method

Situation Nickname:_____

Identify

Describe the situation. Write as much detail as you can.

_____

_____

_____

_____

_____

_____

What are the extreme or all-or-nothing thoughts? Can you identify where they came from? Are you using any identifiers in your internal dialogue?

_____

_____

_____

Challenge

Are you making assumptions? Do you have any facts to back up your thoughts?

_____

_____

_____

What are some middle thinking thoughts you can have? What would you say to a friend if they were in the same situation?

_____

_____

_____

Evaluate

How will replacing the extreme thought with a more balanced one help you reach your goals?

_____

_____

_____

Are there any actions you can take to get out of the extremes? What's stopping you from changing?

_____

_____

_____

ICE Method

Situation Nickname:_____

Identify

Describe the situation. Write as much detail as you can.

_____

_____

_____

_____

_____

_____

What are the extreme or all-or-nothing thoughts? Can you identify where they came from? Are you using any identifiers in your internal dialogue?

_____

_____

_____

Challenge

Are you making assumptions? Do you have any facts to back up your thoughts?

_____

_____

_____

What are some middle thinking thoughts you can have? What would you say to a friend if they were in the same situation?

_____

_____

_____

Evaluate

How will replacing the extreme thought with a more balanced one help you reach your goals?

_____

_____

_____

Are there any actions you can take to get out of the extremes? What's stopping you from changing?

_____

_____

_____

Author's Note

Middle Think is a call to action.

I believe all-or-nothing thinking is the largest contributing factor to today's mental health crisis. Extreme thinking is more than an unhelpful habit; it's a not-so-silent yet invisible killer, causing many people a lot of pain and suffering. It can make you feel hopeless, unloved, and lead to crippling stress, anxiety, and depression—I know, I've been there.

Most people are unknowingly struggling with this destructive habit without the skills to protect themselves. We're unprepared, and it's destroying lives, reducing our shine and dividing us when we need each other most.

I am honored to help you find your path and learn the skills to create a more balanced mindset. See you in The Middle.

Acknowledgements

Thank you to those who share their mental health struggles and to those who are working to gain control of your thoughts. You keep me going.

To my friends for helping me work through my own struggles while writing this book.

To editors and formatters who contributed to this book.

Thank you to my therapist and mental health professionals like Aaron T. Beck.

To my cat for listening to me sing "Meet Me in the Middle" off-key for weeks—not like she had a choice.

And last but not least, thank you to me.

Notes

To keep it conversational, I kept notes to a minimum. Here, you'll find citations for newspaper and magazine articles, reports, blog posts, and online videos. For complete details on books and printed articles, cited by last name(s) and date only, please refer to the References and Recommended Reading section.

1. Burns (1980), p. 28. Burns suggests, "Every bad feeling you have is a result of your distorted negative thinking." While this might be a bit of an exaggeration, there is strong evidence to support that most common mental health challenges stem from seeing the world in all-or-nothing terms.

2. "You just need to toughen up" is an example of all-or-nothing thinking because it oversimplifies complex emotions and challenges into a single solution. It ignores nuance and invalidates emotions, failing to recognize that someone can be upset or offended while still being strong.

3. Reddit user matt_h75. (2024, September 20). *Just found a 1955 newspaper that claims that smoking is harmless*. Reddit. https://www.reddit.com/r/mildlyinteresting/comments/1fl739y/just_found_an_1955_newspaper_that_claims_that/.

4. Snopes. (2024). *Fact check: Did Stephen King tweet that FOX News is responsible for parents' fears of video games?* https://www.snopes.com/fact-check/stephen-king-fox-news-video-games/. I believe that rather than campaigning against video games and violence, efforts should focus on addressing extreme thoughts. This idea is reflected in a tweet that states, "FOX has done to our parents what our parents thought video games would do to us." While this sentiment has been retweeted by Stephen King and others, the original author remains unknown.

5. Gardiner, C. (2024, June 20). *ITS OVER! You'll NEVER afford a home | Housing market update* [Video]. YouTube. https://www.youtube.com/watch?v=0X85P34bYgI. Countless articles suggest that people will "never" be able to afford a house. I chose this YouTube video because it was among the top results when I searched for "You will never buy a house" and is particularly sensationalized. The creator claims that you need a 35% down payment to buy a house, which is an extreme assertion I have not encountered before and cannot find any evidence to support.

Additionally, the video's title features dramatic language, with "ITS OVER!" and "NEVER" in all caps.

6. Daily News. (2020, June 7). *No one is safe.* Cover headline. https://www. facebook.com/story. php?story_fbid=10157354933432541&id=26891427 2540&p=30&_rdr

7. Dubey, S. (2023, March 1). *Looking for love? Bad news – nobody dates to be in relationships anymore.* Huffington Post. https://www.huffingtonpost. co.uk/entry/looking-for-love-bad-news-nobody-dates-to-be-in-relationships-anymore_uk_63f8c7cee4b08b1402dd4acc. This article includes an overwhelming amount of all-or-nothing thinking.

8. Lovato, D. (2017). *Tell me you love me* [Track 2 on *Tell me you love me*]. Westlake Recording.

9. Hendricks, S. (2023, May 24). *Buying a home in today's economy is expensive – but not impossible.* Freethink. https://www.freethink.com/ sponsored/homebuying

10. FBI National Press Office. (2024, June 10). *FBI releases 2024 quarterly crime report and use-of-force data update* https:// www.fbi. gov/news/ press-releases/fbi- releases-2024- quarterly- crime-report-and-use-of-force-data-update

11. Molloy, L. (2024, January 9).*What does dating look like for young people in 2024?* Dazed Digital. https://www.dazeddigital. com/life-culture/ article/61695/1/dating-apps-relationships-young-people-gen-z-love-2024

12. Jacewicz, N. (2017, August 8). *Gnawing questions: Is sugar from fruit the same as sugar from candy?* NPR. https://www.npr.org/sections/ thesalt/2017/08/08/540923229/gnawing-questions-is-sugar-from-fruit-the-same-as-sugar-from-candy

13. Cohen (2022), pp. 78-79.

14. Marti, A. (2019). Ultra-processed foods are not 'real food' but really affect your health. *Nutrients, 11*(8), 1902. https://doi.org/10.3390/ nu11081902

15. Campbell-Danesh, A. (2020, August 31). *Why do most diets fail in the long run?* Psychology Today. https://www.psychologytoday.com/us/blog/ mind-body-food/202008/why-do-most-diets-fail-in-the-long-run

16. Burns (2006), p13.

17. The Editors of Encyclopaedia Britannica. (2010, November 8). *Denial of not-being.* https://www.britannica.com/topic/denial-of-not-being. Philosopher Parmenides argued that there is either being or non-being.

While this is the earliest reference to all-or-nothing thinking I can find, I believe extremes have existed in human thought long before him.

18. Reddit user Meoka2368. (2022, July 20). *Nobody wants to work anymore*. Reddit. https://www.reddit.com/r/antiwork/comments/w3si8l/nobody_wants_to_work_anymore/

19. American Society of Plastic Surgeons. (2018, August 6). Plastic surgery societies issue urgent warning about the risks associated with Brazilian butt lifts. https://www.plasticsurgery.org/news/press-releases/plastic-surgery-societies-issue-urgent-warning-about-the-risks-associated-with-brazilian-butt-lifts. Crime is decreasing while deaths from cosmetic procedures are rising. Yet, when we look at the news or social media, we are often warned to be scared of violence but not informed about the risks of cosmetic procedures.

20. One particularly extreme self-help advocate is David Goggins. His rigid mentality, characterized by a lack of empathy and boundaries, can contribute to burnout.

21. Gao, Y., Liu, F., & Gao, L. (2023). Echo chamber effects on short video platforms. *Scientific Reports*, 13, Article 33370. https://doi.org/10.1038/s41598-023-33370-1

22. While writing *Middle Think*, I commented on an Instagram post claiming that men on dating apps do not respect women. I expressed my frustration with the negativity surrounding dating, noting that while there are undesirables, there are also good men. In response, I was accused of being a man and told that I was probably a rapist.

23. Hu, C. (2024, February 21). Why writing by hand is better for memory and learning. *Scientific American*. https://www.scientificamerican.com/article/why-writing-by-hand-is-better-for-memory-and-learning/

24. Tupy, M. L., & Bailey, R. (2023, March 1). Global murder rate is falling. *Human Progress*. https://humanprogress.org/trends/global-murder-rate-is-falling/

25. Beecham, A. (2024, September). 'Yachting' is about more than being paid to party; it's Hollywood's murkiest open secret. *Stylist*. https://www.stylist.co.uk/long-reads/yachting-hollywood-trafficking/627259

26. Proust (1929), pp. 343-345.

27. Tolle, Eckharte. (1997), p. 48.

28. Greenberger & Padesky (2015), p. 63

29. Stopera, D. (2024, August 20). 50 pictures that prove the American education system is 100% totally and completely doomed. *BuzzFeed*. https://www.buzzfeed.com/daves4/dumb-americans-august-2024

30. Folkenflik, D. (2020, September 29). You literally can't believe the facts Tucker Carlson tells you; so say Fox's lawyers. *NPR.* https://www.npr.org/2020/09/29/917747123/you-literally-cant-believe-the-facts-tucker-carlson-tells-you-so-say-fox-s-lawye

31. Parker, K. (2023, May 22). How Pew Research Center will report on generations moving forward. *Pew Research Center.* https://www.pewresearch.org/short-reads/2023/05/22/how-pew-research-center-will-report-on-generations-moving-forward/

32. Cialdini (2006). pp. 5-12.

33. Rosin, K., & Rosin, C. (Writers). (1992, February 6). *Beverly Hills, 90210* (Season 2, Episode 21: "Everybody's talking 'bout it") [TV series episode]. Directed by D. Attias.

34. Legrand, F. D., Jeandet, P., Beaumont, F., & Polidori, G. (2022). Effects of outdoor walking on positive and negative affect: Nature contact makes a big difference. *Frontiers in Behavioral Neuroscience, 16,* Article 901491. https://doi.org/10.3389/fnbeh.2022.901491

35. Ang, B., Horowitz, M., & Moncrieff, J. (2022). Is the chemical imbalance an 'urban legend'? An exploration of the status of the serotonin theory of depression in the scientific literature. *SSM - Mental Health, 2,* Article 100098. https://doi.org/10.1016/j.ssmmh.2022.100098

36. Pies, R. W. (2019, August 2). Debunking the two chemical imbalance myths, again. *Psychiatric Times, 36*(8). https://www.psychiatrictimes.com/view/debunking-two-chemical-imbalance-myths-again

37. Halpern (2011). p. 253–272.

References and Recommended Reading

Confident and Identity

Cohen, G. L. (2022). *Belonging: The science of creating connection and bridging divides* (1st ed.). New York, NY: W.W. Norton & Company.

Csikszentmihalyi, M. (1990). *Flow: The psychology of optimal experience.* New York, NY: Harper & Row.

Dass, R., & Gorman, P. (1985). *How can I help? Stories and reflections on service.* New York, NY: Alfred A. Knopf.

Wiest, B. (2020). *The mountain is you: Transforming self-sabotage into self-mastery.* New York, NY: Thought Catalog Books.

Thoughts and Therapy

Burns, D.D. (1980). *Feeling good: The new mood therapy.* New York, NY: Avon Books.

Burns, D. D. (2006). *When panic attacks: The new, drug-free anxiety therapy that can change your life.* New York, NY: Harmony.

Greenberger, D., & Padesky, C. A. (2015). *Mind over mood: Change how you feel by changing the way you think.* (2nd ed.). New York, NY: Guilford Publications.

McKay, M., Wood, J.C. & Brantley, J. (2019). *Dialectical behavior therapy skills workbook: Practical DBT exercises for learning mindfulness, interpersonal effectiveness, emotion regulation, and distress tolerance* (2nd ed.). Oakland, CA: New Harbinger Publications.

Mindset and Perspective

Cialdini, R. B. (2006). *Influence: The psychology of persuasion.* New York, NY: Harper Business

Dweck, C. S. (2006). *Mindset: The new psychology of success.* New York, NY: Random House.

Halpern D. F., Beninger A. S., & Straight C. A. (2011). Sex differences in intelligence. In R. J. Sternberg & S. B. Kaufman (Eds.), *The Cambridge handbook of intelligence.* New York, NY: Cambridge University Press.

Kahneman, D. (2011). *Thinking, fast and slow.* New York, NY: Farrar, Straus and Giroux.

Lukianoff, G., & Haidt, J. (2018). *The coddling of the American mind: How good intentions and bad ideas are setting up a generation for failure.* New York, NY: Penguin Press.

Robin, V., & Dominguez, J. (2018). *Your money or your life* (2nd ed.). New York, NY: Penguin Books.

Spirituality and Meaning

Proust, M. (1929). *La prisonnière.* (Vol. 5 of *Remembrance of Things Past,* C. K. Scott Moncrieff, Trans.). New York, NY: Modern Library.

Tolle, E. (1997). *The power of now: A guide to spiritual enlightenment.* Vancouver, Canada: Namaste Publishing.

Trungpa, C. (1973). *Cutting through spiritual materialism.* Boston, MA: Shambhala Publications.

MIDDLE
think

LYNDSEY GETTY

A Book Club Guide

a letter to readers

Hey!

My favorite part of *Middle Think* is the "Meet Me in The Middle" section at the end of "Middle Think Is Unpacking Extremes." I talk about how extreme thinking hinders our ability to find pride and excitement. And my hope is that *Middle Think* inspires you to find the joy and love you deserve.

While I kept it casual here, all-or-nothing thinking is no joke. So be kind to yourself, and know that when you look for The Middle, you will find it.

Thank you so much for reading, and I hope you enjoy discussing your favorite parts of the book.

- Lyndsey

discussion guidelines

These guidelines create a foundation for healthy and thoughtful discussions, while ensuring participants feel supported and respected.

1. **Confidentiality is Key.** What's said in the discussion stays in the discussion. This creates a safe space for all participants to share their thoughts and feelings openly without fear of judgment or gossip.
2. **Respect All Perspectives.** Everyone has different experiences and viewpoints. Listen actively and respectfully, even if you don't agree. Avoid interrupting and make space for others to speak.
3. **No Fixing or Advising.** Unless someone asks for advice, avoid jumping in with solutions. The goal is to share and listen, not to solve or "fix" each other's problems.
4. **Mental Health Awareness.** If someone expresses distress or seems in need of help, gently encourage them to reach out to their therapist or call a mental health hotline (such as the **Suicide & Crisis Lifeline: 988**). The book club is a space for discussion, not professional mental health support.
5. **Nonjudgmental Space.** Avoid judgmental language and tone. This includes refraining from criticizing others' thoughts, opinions, or personal experiences.
6. **Participation Is Encouraged, but Optional.** While everyone is encouraged to participate, it's okay if someone wants to pass on a question or doesn't feel ready to share. Participation should be voluntary and without pressure.

7. **Keep it Constructive.** Constructive discussions help us grow, while negativity can hinder open communication. Focus on productive, thoughtful sharing and be mindful of how your words impact others.

Constructive feedback offers thoughtful and respectful responses creating a supportive environment for discussion. It looks like:

- **Acknowledging contributions**: "I really appreciated your interpretation of that chapter. It made me think differently about the concept."
- **Offering friendly suggestions**: "Could the theme you mentioned be expanded by considering other viewpoints?"
- **Encouraging dialogue**: "What you said was interesting! I'd love to hear more about how you think that connects other areas in the book."

discussion questions

1. What did you know about all-or-nothing thinking and cognitive distortions before reading *Middle Think*?
2. How has all-or-nothing thinking impacted your life? Can you share an example where this mindset held you back?
3. Reflect on the "Unpacking Extremes" section of the book. Were you surprised by the number of extremes present in your surroundings? Think about the people, situations, or even media you engage with daily. How do these extremes influence your thoughts and actions? Did any specific examples from the section resonate with your experiences?
4. When learning your style, where do you find yourself thinking in extremes the most? What steps can you take to foster a more balanced mindset in these areas?
5. Can you identify a recent situation where you experienced all-or-nothing thinking? What were the circumstances, and how did it affect your emotions or decisions?
6. The book discusses the importance of qualifiers in middle thinking. What are some examples of qualifiers you can use in your own thought process to create a more balanced perspective?
7. Share a time when you successfully used middle thinking in a challenging situation. How did it change the outcome or your feelings about the situation?

8. How can focusing on long-term benefits help mitigate the feelings of failure that often come with setbacks? Can you think of a specific goal where this perspective has helped you?

9. Discuss how the people around you affect your thinking. Are there certain individuals who encourage all-or-nothing thinking, and how can you address this?

10. What specific strategies or exercises from the book do you find most helpful for practicing middle thinking? How can you integrate these into your daily routine?

11. Reflect on the statement, "The future is closer than you think." How does this idea resonate with you? In what ways can maintaining a future focus alter your current mindset?

12. What fears or challenges do you face when trying to adopt middle thinking? How can you overcome these obstacles?

13. How do you think practicing middle thinking can impact society as a whole? What changes would you like to see in the discourse around social issues if more people adopted this mindset?

PHOTO BY: Zave Smith

Lyndsey Getty is the founder of The Thought Method Co. and author of the thoughtbook series. She is dedicated to bridging the gap between mental wellness education and practical implementation. A survivor of domestic violence, she adopts a trauma-informed approach and takes pride in not only teaching revolutionary methods but also serving as living proof of their efficacy. She lives in Philadelphia, Pennsylvania.

thoughtmethod.com
@thoughtmethod

Feedback is a gift

Please help others discover *Middle Think* by leaving a review on Amazon

Check out other Thoughtbook titles at thoughtmethod.com

Made in the USA
Las Vegas, NV
15 November 2024

11866027R00075